Everyman's Poetry

Everyman, I will go with thee,
and be thy guide

Lord Byron

Selected and edited by JANE STABLER

University of Dundee

EVERYMAN

J. M. Dent · London

This edition first published by Everyman Paperbacks in 1997
Introduction and other critical apparatus
© J. M. Dent 1997

J. M. Dent
Orion Publishing Group
Orion House
5 Upper St Martin's Lane,
London WC2H 9EA

Typeset by Deltatype Ltd, Birkenhead, Merseyside
Printed in Great Britain by
The Guernsey Press Co. Ltd, Guernsey, C.I.

British Library Cataloguing-in-Publication Data
is available upon request.

ISBN 0 460 87810 7

Contents

Note on the Author and Editor

GEORGE GORDON BYRON was born in 1788 into an unstable second marriage: his father died (or possibly committed suicide) when Byron was two years old and Byron endured a turbulent relationship with his mother until her death while he was away in 1811. After his return to England, the publication of *Childe Harold's Pilgrimage* made the twenty-four-year-old Lord Byron a celebrity in English society – but his fame as an author and a prominent liberal Whig rapidly turned into scandal. Byron rarely saw his half-sister, Augusta, during their childhood but in 1813 they met and fell in love. Attempting to extricate himself from this passion, Byron embarked on a marriage which collapsed publicly after a year amidst rumours of incest. In 1816 Byron left England for ever and went to live in Italy where he was joined by the Shelleys and other exiles from England. From Italy, Byron wrote instalments of *Don Juan*, the epic *ottava rima* poem which his friends, publisher and mistress thought too shocking to publish. Not only in this late satirical work, but throughout his career, Byron's poetic and dramatic writing offers his readers an astonishing variety. From introspective lyrics to risqué sexual comedy, his work is intimately related to his own and to society's preoccupations. His concern for factual precision and for exact verse craftsmanship is at odds with his reputation as a glowering Romantic rebel, but his death in 1824 while active in the struggle to liberate Greece finally allowed him to be reclaimed as a Romantic hero.

JANE STABLER completed her doctoral thesis on Byron's poetry at the University of Glasgow. She is now Lecturer in English at the University of Dundee and is working on a Byron Critical Reader, a study of Transitions in English Romantic Writing 1790–1830, and a study of Byron's modernity.

Chronology of Byron's Life and Times

Year	Life	Historical Events
1788	Born 22 January at Cavendish Square, London, only child of John Byron and his second wife, Catherine Gordon; from his father's first marriage, Byron has a half-sister, Augusta (born 1783)	George III's first attack of madness; bread riots in France
1791	Death of John Byron; moves with Mrs Byron to Aberdeen	Church and King riots in Birmingham; Louis XVI imprisoned
1794	Attends Aberdeen Grammar School	Habeas Corpus suspended; Robespierre guillotined; end of the Terror
1798	Death of grand-uncle, inherits his title; moves with Mrs Byron to Newstead Abbey, Nottingham, the family seat	French invade republican Switzerland to the dismay of English radicals; Irish Rebellion
1801	Becomes a pupil at Harrow School	Napoleon becomes Life Consul
1805	Leads a rebellion against the new headmaster at Harrow; (October) goes into residence at Trinity College, Cambridge	Battle of Trafalgar; Napoleon defeats Russia and Austria at Austerlitz

Year	Life	Historical Events
1807	*Hours of Idleness* published; leaves Cambridge; Augusta marries Colonel George Leigh	France makes the Treaties of Tilsit with Prussia and Russia
1808	*Edinburgh Review* critical of *Hours of Idleness*; begins the satire *English Bards and Scotch Reviewers*	Peninsular War begins between Britain and France in Spain; Britain betrays the Portuguese by the Convention of Cintra
1809	(March) *English Bards and Scotch Reviewers* published; (July) begins tour of the Peninsula and Levant with John Cam Hobhouse; they sail to Portugal, then on to Spain, Malta and Greece; begins *Childe Harold's Pilgrimage*	British victory at Talavera in Spain
1810	Sees the site of Troy and swims from Sestos to Abydos; visits Constantinople with Hobhouse before Hobhouse returns to England; goes to Athens; tours the Morea	Napoleon annexes Holland; George III's insanity is conceded
1811	Drafts *Hints from Horace* and *The Curse of Minerva* (satire on Lord Elgin's removal of marbles from the Parthenon); sails back to England; (August) death of mother and Trinity College friend Charles Skinner Matthews	Luddite rioters near Nottingham begin frame-breaking; George III's madness worsens; Prince of Wales made Regent; Napoleon breaks Treaty of Tilsit and alienates Russia

Year	Life	Historical Events
1812	(February) Delivers his maiden speech (supporting the frame-breakers) in the House of Lords; (March) publication of *Childe Harold's Pilgrimage* Cantos I and II makes him famous: Coleridge writes, 'All the world is talking of it'; (September) begins *The Giaour*	Luddite riots spread across the Midlands and north of England; final shipment of Elgin marbles arrives in England; (September) Napoleon enters Moscow but is forced to retreat by the winter weather
1813	(May) Visits Leigh Hunt who is in prison for libelling the Prince Regent; (June) *The Giaour* published; (August) affair with Augusta intensifies; produces a succession of hugely popular oriental tales in verse	Mass Luddite trials; many executions; Wellington drives the French out of Spain; Napoleon is defeated at the Battle of Leipzig
1814	Works on *Hebrew Melodies*	Allies invade France; Napoleon is exiled to Elba
1815	(2 January) Marries Annabella Milbanke and they settle in London; joins the management subcommittee of the Drury Lane Theatre (a Whig project); (10 December) birth of Augusta Ada Byron	Napoleon marches on Paris and assumes the position of Emperor again; Wellington defeats Napoleon at Waterloo; Napoleon abdicates and is banished to St Helena; Wellington is lauded as a national hero
1816	(January) Lady Byron leaves the London house, taking Ada with her, and begins separation	Economic depression follows the end of the Napoleonic Wars; Spa Fields Riot in London

Year	Life	Historical Events
	proceedings; Byron hopes for reconciliation but scandalous rumours banish him from London society; (April) leaves England for ever; begins *Childe Harold's Pilgrimage* Canto III; (May) travels from Waterloo along the Rhine to Switzerland where he meets Percy Shelley, Mary Godwin and Claire Clairmont; tours with Shelley round Lake Geneva; (August) Shelley's party returns to England; Claire is pregnant with Byron's child; visited by Hobhouse and they tour the Alps together; (September) begins *Manfred*; (October) begins with Hobhouse a tour of Italy and they arrive in Venice in November; Canto III of *CHP* published	
1817	(12 January) Birth of Allegra, illegitimate daughter of Byron and Claire; bases himself in Venice; (April–May) visits Rome; (June) *Manfred*	Walter Scott reviews *CHP* III in the *Quarterly Review*; the poem prompts much discussion about Byron's mental state; death of Princess Charlotte; suspension of Habeas Corpus as civil unrest continues

Year	Life	Historical Events
	published; works on *Childe Harold's Pilgrimage* Canto IV and *Beppo*; (December) Newstead Abbey sold	
1818	(February) *Beppo* published anonymously; (April) *CHP* IV published; (July) begins *Don Juan*	(January) Habeas Corpus restored; defeat of Burdett's motion for parliamentary reform
1819	(April) Begins a long affair with Teresa Guiccioli; (June–September) visits her in Ravenna; (July) *Don Juan* Cantos I–II published; (October–November) works on *Don Juan* Canto III; (December) leaves Venice again for Ravenna	(August) Peterloo Massacre, Manchester; parliament passes the Six Acts to suppress demonstrations of public unrest
1820	(March) resumes work on the satire *Hints from Horace* in the context of his defence of Alexander Pope's poetry against the style of the Lake School Poets and John Keats; begins work on historical dramas and becomes involved with Italian revolutionaries; (November) involved in the aftermath of a shooting incident in Ravenna	(January) Death of George III; accession of Prince Regent as George IV who attempts to divorce and discredit Queen Caroline; her cause becomes a focus for popular discontent; reports of the Cato Street Conspiracy horrify Byron in Italy; revolution begins in Spain; the revolt led by the Carbonari in Naples begins but is crushed by the Austrians in 1821

Year	Life	Historical Events
1821	Purchases and stores arms for the Carbonari, continues work on historical dramas and begins *Cain*, a sceptical Mystery play; Teresa apparently asks him to stop writing *Don Juan*; (August) visited by Shelley in Ravenna; *Don Juan* Cantos III–V published; responds to Robert Southey's attack on him by writing *The Vision of Judgement*; (November) settles in Pisa near the Shelleys	Death of Keats in Rome; Byron retracts his criticism of Keats; (May) Lord John Russell's motion for parliamentary reform is rejected; death of Napoleon on St Helena; (July) lavish coronation of George IV; (August) death of Queen Caroline; Greek War of Independence against the Turks begins
1822	Resumes work on *Don Juan*; growing tension with Murray about the future of *Don Juan*; Murray faces outcry for publishing *Cain*; (April) Allegra dies from fever in the convent where Byron had placed her; (July) Leigh Hunt arrives with his family to work on a new journal, *The Liberal*, with Byron and Shelley; Shelley is drowned while sailing his boat, the *Don Juan*; Byron helps to support Mary Shelley	Greek independence proclaimed; British Foreign Secretary, Castlereagh, commits suicide; Tory cabinet is joined by liberals Peel and Canning

Year	Life	Historical Events
	and the Hunts; (October) the first number of *The Liberal* appears including *The Vision of Judgement* for which the publisher, John Hunt, is prosecuted; continues work on *Don Juan* and withdraws from Murray as publisher, telling him to pass over unpublished poems to John Hunt	
1823	(April) Is invited to become a member of the London Greek Committee; (July) *Don Juan* Cantos VI–VIII published by Hunt; leaves Italy for Greece; (August) arrives in Cephalonia; *Don Juan* Cantos IX–XI published by Hunt; receives visits from many people who wish to be involved in the Greek cause; arranges financial backing for the Greek Provisional Government; (December) *Don Juan* Cantos XII–XIV published by Hunt; sails to Missolonghi	Robert Peel begins series of penal reforms
1824	(January) John Hunt stands trial for publishing *The Vision*	Repeal of the Combinations Act enables the foundation of trades unions; foundation of the

Year	Life	Historical Events
	of Judgement; (February) earthquake in Missolonghi; (March) *Don Juan* Cantos XV–XVI published by Hunt; (April) while riding, is caught in a rainstorm and develops a fever; against his wishes, is bled by doctors and his condition worsens; requests that his body should be left in Greece 'without pomp or nonsense'; dies 19 April; at the end of April his remains are sent to England	RSPCA; (May) Byron's memoirs are burned in Murray's office; (July) funeral procession takes Byron's coffin from London to Nottingham where he is buried in the family vault at Hucknall Torkard

Introduction

Born on 22 January 1788, George Gordon Byron was ten and a half years old when Wordsworth's and Coleridge's *Lyrical Ballads* first appeared. By the time Byron was twenty-one Wordsworth and Coleridge were established literary figures who had abandoned their revolutionary ideals for conservative values. Byron's background allied him with the ruling class: he had been brought up in Scotland, sent to Harrow School, inherited a peerage, and passed through Trinity College, Cambridge but (unlike the authors of *Lyrical Ballads*) he sustained an imaginative capacity to sympathise with marginalised individuals. Aged nineteen he published *Hours of Idleness*, a collection of poems showing flickers of keen satirical intelligence, but also a certain amount of lordly posturing. When the pretensions of this volume were pointed out in the *Edinburgh Review*, Byron changed his style and countered with a satire, *English Bards and Scotch Reviewers*, which assailed not only Scottish reviewers but most of the English literary and political establishment. He then left England for a long continental tour.

Byron's letters and the journal kept by his companion John Cam Hobhouse give a stimulating account of this journey around Spain, Portugal, Malta, Albania and Greece (1809–11). His letters display a zest for travel and an appetite for new experiences: 'I am very happy here,' he wrote from Lisbon to a friend, 'because I loves oranges, and talk bad Latin to the monks, who understand it, as it is like their own, – and I goes into society (with my pocket-pistols), and I swims in the Tagus all across at once, and I rides on an ass or a mule, and swears Portuguese, and have got a diarrhoea and bites from the mosquitoes. But what of that? Comfort must not be expected by folks that go a pleasuring***.' (The rest of this paragraph was expurgated by the friend who first collected and edited Byron's letters.)[1]

An unrestrained pursuit of all activities on offer involved Byron in the usual sightseeing, and also literary translation, probable espionage, over-eating, consequent fasting, plus various infectious diseases. His letters use a variety of voices to dramatise these exploits for different audiences. Verse, too, was a means of responding to particular circumstances with a specific verbal shape as we can see in the various *envois* or 'farewells' which Byron produced. 'Farewell to Hobhouse' parodies the conventional loving itemisation of valediction by substituting a list of shared frustrations and embarrassments. By contrast, Byron composed a lilting farewell for the hero of *Childe Harold's Pilgrimage*:

> Adieu, adieu! my native shore
>> Fades o'er the waters blue;
> The Night-winds sigh, the breakers roar,
>> And shrieks the wild seamew.
> Yon Sun that sets upon the sea
>> We follow in his flight;
> Farewell awhile to him and thee,
>> My native Land – Good Night.

The sentimental archaism of 'Yon Sun' almost invites us to consider this lyric as a parody too, but it was received by Byron's contemporaries as one of the most poignant verses in the poem. Uncertainty about how much irony underlies such moments is one of the many destabilising experiences of reading Byron's verse. His ability to shift register and tone not just between poems, but sometimes within the same poem, proved to be a disturbing characteristic for his readers.

Throughout his time abroad, Byron experimented with verse. He began a sequel to his satire (*Hints from Horace*) which continued to exalt Dryden and Pope above the generation of 'Lake School Poets' – Wordsworth, Coleridge and Southey (later Byron would add the 'tadpole' Keats to this group). Although Byron could offer generous praise of some of his contemporaries (Shelley, for example), his preference for neo-classical craftsmanship placed him at odds with the taste of his time. His ambiguous feelings about self-expression still surprise modern readers for whom the adjective 'Byronic' signifies only the rebellious figure whose influence permeates nineteenth-century European literature, art and music.

The cult of the 'Byronic hero' originated in *Childe Harold's Pilgrimage*, the second long poem Byron wrote while abroad. This work – part travelogue and part Spenserian romance – starred a misanthropic and restless hero with a prematurely jaded view of nature and society. On Byron's return to England, both poems were entrusted to a literary adviser; the satire was shelved but *Childe Harold* was published on 10 March 1812 by John Murray. It sold out in three days.

The lyrical reflections of the poet-hero on refugees, battlefields, the ruined cities of Europe under Napoleon, and Greece under Turkish rule were wildly popular. Quotable passages of melancholy were, however, interspersed with comments of a more specific nature on the effects of British domestic and foreign policy. In particular, Byron drew his readers' attention to British military and diplomatic blunders and to a shameful similarity between contemporary oppression of the Greeks and the suffering of Irish Catholics. Many of the reviewers objected to this tendency and regretted that 'Lord Byron should have gone out of his way to dwell . . . on an event which, at least, *he* conceives to have been disgraceful to his country.' Regarding Byron's comments on the Irish Catholics, a writer for the *British Review* accused Byron of 'indulging in comparisons which his excellent sense must feel to be unfounded, and which are too preposterously violent for declamation, or even poetry to adopt'. This controversy enhanced the fashionable glamour of both poem and poet.

Between 1812 and 1815 Byron's public profile was high. His speeches in the House of Lords marked him as a liberal Whig, and he contributed to the opposition party in a number of ways, including his membership of the management subcommittee for the Drury Lane Theatre (one of Lord Holland's projects). Reading the scripts of hundreds of new plays submitted to the committee sharpened his awareness of the taste of English audiences and his own poetry nurtured the growth of sensational melodrama. Following the success of *Childe Harold's Pilgrimage*, Byron produced a succession of verse narratives which squeezed Walter Scott's popularity, and gratified the English readers' demand for crime and passion in Eastern settings.

Byron lived on credit between London and his country residence at Newstead Abbey in Nottinghamshire, and fell into a number of risky high-society sexual liaisons. Transgression became part of his complex poetic identity. Reviewers and social commentators transposed the contradictory qualities of his oriental heroes on to the poet himself. As Maria Edgeworth noted in a letter of 8 September 1818: 'Madame de Staël saw a good deal of Lord Byron at Coppet and said that there is one striking characteristic resemblance between his countenance and Buonaparte's – that the different parts of the physiognomy never agreed in expression. When the mouth smiled the eyes did not smile.'[2]

While still in his twenties, Byron had become an idol and then, just as rapidly, an outcast of English society. In summer 1813 Byron's sexual relationship with his half-sister, Augusta Leigh, produced a personal crisis which was to have wider public implications. Byron married Annabella Milbanke in 1815, albeit with some reluctance. The marriage broke down after a year. Byron left England in 1816 to escape rumours about his separation and never returned. His daughter, Ada, was not yet a year old. As Byron left, creditors moved in to repossess his apartments in Piccadilly.

The separation scandal made a lasting impact on Byron's writing. His bitterness about the failure of his marriage found an outlet in poetry which addressed his wife and her supporters directly or which used allusive hints for those readers familiar with their domestic circumstances. 'Endorsement to the Deed of Separation', 'Fare Thee Well!' and *Childe Harold* Canto III are all responses to the public collapse of his private life – although the third Canto of *Childe Harold* is also another attempt on Byron's part to overpower the Lake School, using sublime Alpine scenery to mirror his rejection of human society.

In Switzerland in 1816 Byron met Percy and Mary Shelley and re-encountered Claire Clairmont. Care of the child Claire and Byron conceived that summer was one of the complicating factors in Byron's relationship with the Shelleys, but they shared their exile in Italy together. Philosophically, Byron and Percy Shelley had different outlooks: whereas Shelley's Platonism informed his radical politics with the hope of an ideal world in the future, Byron's sceptical, materialist inclinations undermined the idea of a hidden meaning in the universe. Isolation and guilt were accepted by his readers as very poetical circumstances, but Byron's hints that moral order was entirely relative, and that religion created a false (because systematic) unity, outraged the more orthodox members of the public: 'The mischief that lurks in all Lord Byron's productions', according to the *British Review*, is that 'they bring qualities of a most contradictory kind into close alliance; and so shape them into seeming union as to confound sentiments, which, for the sake of sound morality and social security, should forever be kept contrasted'.

By 1817, Byron's experiments with verse form were turning his poetry towards the immediate texture of human existence. He completed the fourth Canto of *Childe Harold's Pilgrimage* and within months began to compose *Beppo: A Venetian Story*, using the Italian *ottava rima* stanza. *Beppo* does tell a story, but one which is interrupted continuously with conversational asides on whatever catches the narrator's attention. This apparently effortless digressive technique allowed Byron to juxtapose different moods and subjects while remaining within a tight rhyme scheme. The humour wrong-footed some of Byron's most hostile critics (partly because first editions appeared anonymously) but others were not slow to trace connections between the changeable voice in this and Byron's earlier poems: '*Beppo* is by no means inconsistent with the peculiar bent of his wild and wayward genius', claimed the *Scots Magazine*.

In July 1818 Byron began a new poem – *Don Juan* – whose mock-epic proportions allowed even more scope for conversational asides. The range of subject matter was bold, mixing romantic adventures and sexual comedy with scathing topical satire. Byron's friends and his publisher feared that the poem's overt political references and oblique personal ones would cause a scandal. Byron resisted all attempts to suppress the poem and when the first Cantos were published (anonymously, though recognisable as Byron's) there was the expected outcry. *Don Juan* was seen as a 'prostitution' of Byron's genius all the more pernicious because the 'wickedness' of the poem was inextricably mingled with its 'beauty and grace'.

In recent years there have been notable reassessments of Byron's work. Critics have argued that Byron's reputation as a freedom-fighter is more of a rhetorical pose than a reality: he remained, after all, intensely proud of his status as a British peer, and was appalled by the Cato Street Conspiracy. His anti-feminine jokes in letters and poems are insultingly obvious. Byron's sustained unsettlement of our complacencies, however, offers much more potential for free thought and remains the source of his distinctive strength and vitality as a poet. After five Cantos of *Don Juan*, Murray refused to issue any more of the poem and Byron had to turn to the notorious radical publisher John Hunt. Canto XVII was found, unfinished, among Byron's papers at his death. *Don Juan* continues to be a source of controversy: should we read it as epic or fragment, reactionary or radical, picaresque or post-modern, unified by a personality or joyfully disorganised, optimistic or bitterly cynical? The poem's shimmering surface changes with every reader and with every reading, justifying Byron's defence of it in 1819: 'you are all right – and I am all wrong – but do pray let me have that pleasure'.[3]

It is to the pleasure of reading Byron, even in extracts, that this selection from his poetry is dedicated.

JANE STABLER

References

1 *Byron's Letters and Journals*, I, 215
2 Maria Edgeworth, *Letters from England 1813–1844*, ed. Christina Colvin (Oxford: Clarendon Press, 1971), p. 84.
3 BLJ, VI, 206–7.

Note on the Text

This selection is based on the standard edition of Byron's *Complete Poetical Works* edited by Jerome J. McGann (Oxford: Clarendon Press, 1980–93) with some corrections. I am grateful to John Murray for permission to include lines omitted from the *Complete Poetical Works*. I am grateful to Nicholas Roe and Peter Cochran for general editorial advice.

Lord Byron

Inscription on the Monument of a Newfoundland Dog

Near this spot
Are deposited the Remains of one
Who possessed Beauty without Vanity,
Strength without Insolence,
Courage without Ferocity,
And all the Virtues of Man without his Vices.
This Praise, which would be unmeaning Flattery
If inscribed over human ashes,
Is but a just tribute to the Memory of
BOATSWAIN, a Dog,
Who was born at Newfoundland, May, 1803,
And died at Newstead Abbey, Nov. 18, 1808.

When some proud son of man returns to earth,
Unknown to glory, but upheld by birth,
The sculptor's art exhausts the pomp of woe,
And storied urns record who rests below;
When all is done, upon the tomb is seen,
Not what he was, but what he should have been:
But the poor dog, in life the firmest friend,
The first to welcome, foremost to defend,
Whose honest heart is still his master's own,
Who labours, fights, lives, breathes for him alone,   10
Unhonoured falls, unnoticed all his worth,
Denied in heaven the soul he held on earth:
While man, vain insect! hopes to be forgiven,
And claims himself a sole exclusive heaven.
Oh man! thou feeble tenant of an hour,
Debased by slavery, or corrupt by power,
Who knows thee well must quit thee with disgust,
Degraded mass of animated dust!
Thy love is lust, thy friendship all a cheat,

Thy smiles hypocrisy, thy words deceit!   20
By nature vile, ennobled but by name,
Each kindred brute might bid thee blush for shame.
Ye! who perchance behold this simple urn,
Pass on – it honours none you wish to mourn:
To mark a friend's remains these stones arise,
I never knew but one, and here he lies.

Farewell Petition to
J[ohn] C[am] H[obhouse] Esq.

Oh thou yclep'd by vulgar sons of men
Cam Hobhouse! but by wags Byzantian Ben!
Twin sacred titles, which combined appear
To grace thy volume's front, and gild its rear,
Since now thou put'st thyself and work to Sea
And leav'st all Greece to *Fletcher* and to me,
Oh hear my single muse our sorrows tell,
One song for *self*, and Fletcher quite as well. –

First to the *Castle* of that man of woes
Dispatch the letter which *I must* enclose;   10
And when his lone Penelope shall say,
Why, where, and *wherefore* doth my William stay?
Spare not to move her pity, or her pride –
By all that Hero suffered, or defied;
The *chicken's toughness*, and the *lack* of *Ale*,
The *stoney mountain*, and the *miry vale*,
The *Garlick* steams, which *half* his meals enrich,
The *impending vermin*, and the *threatened Itch*;
That *ever-breaking* Bed, beyond repair!
The hat too *old*, the coat too *cold* to wear;   20

The hunger, *which, repulsed from Sally's door*,
Pursues her grumbling half from shore to shore;

The Vizier's galliot, and Albania's rocks
All Asia's bugs and Pera's sable Pox: —
Be these the themes to greet his faithful Rib,
So may thy pen be smooth, thy tongue be glib!

This duty done let me in turn demand
Some friendly office in my native land;
Yet let me ponder well, before I ask,
And set thee swearing at the tedious task.   30

First the Miscellany! — to Southwell town
Per coach for Mrs. *Pigot* frank it down;
So may'st thou prosper in the paths of Sale,
And Longman smirk and critics cease to rail.

All hail to Matthews! wash his reverend feet,
And in my name the man of Method greet,
Tell him, my guide, Philosopher, and Friend,
Who cannot love me, and who will not mend,
Tell him, that not in vain I shall essay
To tread and trace our 'old Horatian way',   40
And be (with prose supply my dearth of rhymes)
What better men have been in better times.

Here let me cease, for why should I prolong
My notes, and vex a *Singer* with a *Song*?
Oh thou with pen perpetual in thy fist!
Dubbed for thy sins a stark Miscellanist,
So pleased the printer's orders to perform,
For Messrs. *Longman, Hurst,* and *Rees* and *Orme,*
Go, get thee hence to Paternoster Row,
Thy patrons wave a duodecimo!   50
(Best form for *letters* from a distant land,
It fits the pocket, nor fatigues the hand.)
Then go, once more the joyous work commence
With stores of anecdote, and grains of sense.
Oh may Mammas relent, and Sires forgive!

And scribbling Sons grow dutiful and live!
                    Constantinople, 7 June 1810

To Inez

1

Nay, smile not at my sullen brow,
    Alas! I cannot smile again;
Yet heaven avert that ever thou
    Shouldst weep, and haply weep in vain.

2

And dost thou ask, what secret woe
    I bear, corroding joy and youth?
And wilt thou vainly seek to know
    A pang, ev'n thou must fail to soothe?

3

It is not love, it is not hate,
    Nor low Ambition's honours lost,   10
That bids me loathe my present state,
    And fly from all I priz'd the most:

4

It is that weariness which springs
    From all I meet, or hear, or see:
To me no pleasure Beauty brings;
    Thine eyes have scarce a charm for me.

5

It is that settled, ceaseless gloom
    The fabled Hebrew wanderer bore;
That will not look beyond the tomb,
    But cannot hope for rest before.   20

6

What Exile from himself can flee?
    To Zones, though more and more remote,

Still, still pursues, where-e'er I be,
    The blight of life – the demon, Thought.

7

Yet others rapt in pleasure seem,
    And taste of all that I forsake;
Oh! may they still of transport dream,
    And ne'er, at least like me, awake!

8

Through many a clime 'tis mine to go,
    With many a retrospection curst;   30
And all my solace is to know,
    Whate'er betides, I've known the worst.

9

What is that worst? Nay do not ask –
    In pity from the search forbear:
Smile on – nor venture to unmask
    Man's heart, and view the Hell that's there.

Stanzas For Music

I speak not – I trace not – I breathe not thy name,
There is grief in the sound – there were guilt in the fame;
But the tear which now burns on my cheek may impart
The deep thought that dwells in that silence of heart.

Too brief for our passion, too long for our peace,
Were those hours, can their joy or their bitterness cease?
We repent – we abjure – we will break from our chain;
We must part – we must fly to – unite it again.

Oh! thine be the gladness and mine be the guilt,
Forgive me adored one – forsake if thou wilt;   10

But the heart which I bear shall expire undebased,
And man shall not break it – whatever thou may'st.

And stern to the haughty, but humble to thee,
My soul in its bitterest blackness shall be;
And our days seem as swift – and our moments more sweet,
With thee by my side – than the world at our feet.

One sigh of thy sorrow – one look of thy love,
Shall turn me or fix, shall reward or reprove;
And the heartless may wonder at all we resign,
Thy lip shall reply not to them – but to mine.   20

She Walks in Beauty

1

She walks in beauty, like the night
   Of cloudless climes and starry skies;
And all that's best of dark and bright
   Meet in her aspect and her eyes:
Thus mellow'd to that tender light
   Which heaven to gaudy day denies.

2

One shade the more, one ray the less,
   Had half impair'd the nameless grace
Which waves in every raven tress,
   Or softly lightens o'er her face;   10
Where thoughts serenely sweet express
   How pure, how dear their dwelling place.

3

And on that cheek, and o'er that brow,
   So soft, so calm, yet eloquent,
The smiles that win, the tints that glow,
   But tell of days in goodness spent,

A mind at peace with all below,
A heart whose love is innocent!

The Destruction of Semnacherib

1

The Assyrian came down like the wolf on the fold,
And his cohorts were gleaming in purple and gold;
And the sheen of their spears was like stars on the sea,
When the blue wave rolls nightly on deep Galilee.

2

Like the leaves of the forest when Summer is green,
That host with their banners at sunset were seen:
Like the leaves of the forest when Autumn hath blown,
That host on the morrow lay withered and strown.

3

For the Angel of Death spread his wings on the blast,
And breathed in the face of the foe as he pass'd;   10
And the eyes of the sleepers wax'd deadly and chill,
And their hearts but once heaved, and for ever grew still!

4

And there lay the steed with his nostril all wide,
But through it there roll'd not the breath of his pride:
And the foam of his gasping lay white on the turf,
And cold as the spray of the rock-beating surf.

5

And there lay the rider distorted and pale,
With the dew on his brow, and the rust on his mail;
And the tents were all silent, the banners alone,
The lances unlifted, the trumpet unblown.   20

6

And the widows of Ashur are loud in their wail,
And the idols are broke in the temple of Baal;
And the might of the Gentile, unsmote by the sword,
Hath melted like snow in the glance of the Lord!

When We Two Parted

1

When we two parted
    In silence and tears,
Half broken-hearted
    To sever for years,
Pale grew thy cheek and cold,
    Colder thy kiss;
Truly that hour foretold
    Sorrow to this.

2

The dew of the morning
    Sunk chill on my brow –
It felt like the warning
    Of what I feel now.   10
Thy vows are all broken,
    And light is thy fame;
I hear thy name spoken,
    And share in its shame.

3

They name thee before me,
    A knell to mine ear;
A shudder comes o'er me –
    Why wert thou so dear?   20
They know not I knew thee,
    Who knew thee too well: –

Long, long shall I rue thee,
  Too deeply to tell.

4

In secret we met –
  In silence I grieve,
That thy heart could forget,
  Thy spirit deceive.
If I should meet thee
  After long years,   30
How should I greet thee! –
  With silence and tears.

Fare Thee Well!

Alas! they had been friends in Youth;
But whispering tongues can poison truth;
And constancy lives in realms above;
And Life is thorny; and youth is vain;
And to be wroth with one we love,
Doth work like madness in the brain;
  *   *   *   *   *   *   *   *   *   *   *
But never either found another
To free the hollow heart from paining –
They stood aloof, the scars remaining,
Like cliffs, which had been rent asunder;
A dreary sea now flows between,
But neither heat, nor frost, nor thunder
Shall wholly do away, I ween,
The marks of that which once hath been.

Coleridge, *Christabel*, 408–13, 419–26.

Fare thee well! and if for ever –
  Still for ever, fare *thee well* –
Even though unforgiving, never
  'Gainst thee shall my heart rebel. –

Would that breast were bared before thee
   Where thy head so oft hath lain,
While that placid sleep came o'er thee
   Which thou ne'er can'st know again:
Would that breast by thee glanc'd over,
   Every inmost thought could show!   10
Then, thou would'st at last discover
   'Twas not well to spurn it so –
Though the world for this commend thee –
   Though it smile upon the blow,
Even its praises must offend thee,
   Founded on another's woe –
Though my many faults defaced me,
   Could no other arm be found
Than the one which once embraced me,
   To inflict a cureless wound!   20
Yet – oh, yet – thyself deceive not –
   Love may sink by slow decay,
But by sudden wrench, believe not,
   Hearts can thus be torn away;
Still thine own its life retaineth –
   Still must mine – though bleeding – beat,
And the undying thought which paineth
   Is – that we no more may meet. –
These are words of deeper sorrow
   Than the wail above the dead,   30
Both shall live – but every morrow
   Wake us from a widowed bed. –
And when thou wouldst solace gather –
   When our child's first accents flow –
Wilt thou teach her to say – 'Father!'
   Though his care she must forego?
When her little hands shall press thee –
   When her lip to thine is prest –
Think of him whose prayer shall bless thee –
   Think of him thy love had bless'd.   40
Should her lineaments resemble
   Those thou never more may'st see –
Then thy heart will softly tremble
   With a pulse yet true to me. –

All my faults – perchance thou knowest –
    All my madness – none can know;
All my hopes – where'er thou goest –
    Wither – yet with *thee* they go. –
Every feeling hath been shaken,
    Pride – which not a world could bow –   50
Bows to thee – by thee forsaken
    Even my soul forsakes me now. –
But 'tis done – all words are idle –
    Words from me are vainer still;
But the thoughts we cannot bridle
    Force their way without the will. –
Fare thee well! – thus disunited –
    Torn from every nearer tie –
Seared in heart – and lone – and blighted –
    More than this, I scarce can die.   60

Endorsement to the Deed of
Separation, in the April of 1816

A year ago you swore, fond she!
    'To love, to honour', and so forth:
Such was the vow you pledged to me,
    And here's exactly what 'tis worth.

from **Childe Harold's Pilgrimage**

Canto III

Afin que cette application vous forçât à penser à autre chose.
Il n'y a en vérité de remède que celui-là et le temps.

Lettre du Roi de Prusse à D'Alembert, 7 September 1776.

1

Is thy face like thy mother's, my fair child!
Ada! sole daughter of my house and heart?
When last I saw thy young blue eyes they smiled,
And then we parted, – not as now we part,
But with a hope. –
　　　　　　Awakening with a start,
The waters heave around me; and on high
The winds lift up their voices: I depart,
Whither I know not; but the hour's gone by,
When Albion's lessening shores could grieve or glad mine eye.

2

Once more upon the waters! yet once more!　　　　　　10
And the waves bound beneath me as a steed
That knows his rider. Welcome, to their roar!
Swift be their guidance, wheresoe'er it lead!
Though the strain'd mast should quiver as a reed,
And the rent canvas fluttering strew the gale,
Still must I on; for I am as a weed,
Flung from the rock, on Ocean's foam, to sail
Where'er the surge may sweep, or tempest's breath prevail.

3

In my youth's summer I did sing of One,
The wandering outlaw of his own dark mind;　　　　　　20
Again I seize the theme then but begun,
And bear it with me, as the rushing wind
Bears the cloud onwards: in that Tale I find
The furrows of long thought, and dried-up tears,
Which, ebbing, leave a sterile track behind,

O'er which all heavily the journeying years
Plod the last sands of life, – where not a flower appears.

4

Since my young days of passion – joy, or pain,
Perchance my heart and harp have lost a string,
And both may jar: it may be, that in vain   30
I would essay as I have sung to sing.
Yet, though a dreary strain, to this I cling;
So that it wean me from the weary dream
Of selfish grief or gladness – so it fling
Forgetfulness around me – it shall seem
To me, though to none else, a not ungrateful theme.

5

He, who grown aged in this world of woe,
In deeds, not years, piercing the depths of life,
So that no wonder waits him; nor below
Can love, or sorrow, fame, ambition, strife,   40
Cut to his heart again with the keen knife
Of silent, sharp endurance: he can tell
Why thought seeks refuge in lone caves, yet rife
With airy images, and shapes which dwell
Still unimpair'd, though old, in the soul's haunted cell.

6

'Tis to create, and in creating live
A being more intense, that we endow
With form our fancy, gaining as we give
The life we image, even as I do now.
What am I? Nothing; but not so art thou,   50
Soul of my thought! with whom I traverse earth,
Invisible but gazing, as I glow
Mix'd with thy spirit, blended with thy birth,
And feeling still with thee in my crush'd feelings' dearth.

7

Yet must I think less wildly: – I *have* thought
Too long and darkly, till my brain became,
In its own eddy boiling and o'erwrought,

A whirling gulf of phantasy and flame:
And thus, untaught in youth my heart to tame,
My springs of life were poison'd. 'Tis too late!   60
Yet am I chang'd; though still enough the same
In strength to bear what time can not abate,
And feed on bitter fruits without accusing Fate. [...]

15

But in Man's dwellings he became a thing
Restless and worn, and stern and wearisome,
Droop'd as a wild-born falcon with clipt wing,
To whom the boundless air alone were home:
Then came his fit again, which to o'ercome,   130
As eagerly the barr'd-up bird will beat
His breast and beak against his wiry dome
Till the blood tinge his plumage, so the heat
Of his impeded soul would through his bosom eat.

16

Self-exiled Harold wanders forth again,
With nought of hope left, but with less of gloom;
The very knowledge that he lived in vain,
That all was over on this side the tomb,
Had made Despair a smilingness assume,   140
Which, though 'twere wild, – as on the plundered wreck
When mariners would madly meet their doom
With draughts intemperate on the sinking deck, –
Did yet inspire a cheer, which he forbore to check.

17

Stop! – for thy tread is on an Empire's dust!
An Earthquake's spoil is sepulchred below!
Is the spot mark'd with no colossal bust?
Nor column trophied for triumphal show?
None; but the moral's truth tells simpler so,
As the ground was before, thus let it be; –   150
How that red rain hath made the harvest grow!
And is this all the world has gained by thee,
Thou first and last of fields! king-making Victory?

18

And Harold stands upon this place of skulls,
The grave of France, the deadly Waterloo!
How in an hour the power which gave annuls
Its gifts, transferring fame as fleeting too!
In 'pride of place' here last the eagle flew,
Then tore with bloody talon the rent plain,
Pierced by the shaft of banded nations through;   160
Ambition's life and labours all were vain;
He wears the shattered links of the world's broken chain.

19

Fit retribution! Gaul may champ the bit
And foam in fetters; – but is Earth more free?
Did nations combat to make *One* submit;
Or league to teach all kings true sovereignty?
What! shall reviving Thraldom again be
The patched-up idol of enlightened days?
Shall we, who struck the Lion down, shall we
Pay the Wolf homage? proffering lowly gaze   170
And servile knees to thrones? No; *prove* before ye praise!

20

If not, o'er one fallen despot boast no more!
In vain fair cheeks were furrowed with hot tears
For Europe's flowers long rooted up before
The trampler of her vineyards; in vain years
Of death, depopulation, bondage, fears,
Have all been borne, and broken by the accord
Of roused-up millions: all that most endears
Glory, is when the myrtle wreathes a sword   180
Such as Harmodius drew on Athens' tyrant lord.

21

There was a sound of revelry by night,
And Belgium's capital had gathered then
Her Beauty and her Chivalry, and bright
The lamps shone o'er fair women and brave men;
A thousand hearts beat happily; and when
Music arose with its voluptuous swell,
Soft eyes look'd love to eyes which spake again,

And all went merry as a marriage-bell;
But hush! hark! a deep sound strikes like a rising knell!

22

Did ye not hear it? — No; 'twas but the wind,   190
Or the car rattling o'er the stony street;
On with the dance! let joy be unconfined;
No sleep till morn, when Youth and Pleasure meet
To chase the glowing Hours with flying feet —
But, hark! — that heavy sound breaks in once more,
As if the clouds its echo would repeat;
And nearer, clearer, deadlier than before!
Arm! Arm! and out — it is — the cannon's opening roar!

23

Within a windowed niche of that high hall
Sate Brunswick's fated chieftain; he did hear   200
That sound the first amidst the festival,
And caught its tone with Death's prophetic ear;
And when they smiled because he deem'd it near,
His heart more truly knew that peal too well
Which stretch'd his father on a bloody bier,
And roused the vengeance blood alone could quell:
He rush'd into the field, and, foremost fighting, fell.

24

Ah! then and there was hurrying to and fro,
And gathering tears, and tremblings of distress,
And cheeks all pale, which but an hour ago   210
Blush'd at the praise of their own loveliness;
And there were sudden partings, such as press
The life from out young hearts, and choking sighs
Which ne'er might be repeated; who could guess
If ever more should meet those mutual eyes,
Since upon nights so sweet such awful morn could rise?

25

And there was mounting in hot haste: the steed,
The mustering squadron, and the clattering car,
Went pouring forward in impetuous speed,

And swiftly forming in the ranks of war;   220
And the deep thunder peal on peal afar;
And near, the beat of the alarming drum
Roused up the soldier ere the morning star; ·
While throng'd the citizens with terror dumb,
Or whispering, with white lips – 'The foe! They come! they
    come!'

26

And wild and high the 'Cameron's gathering' rose!
The war-note of Lochiel, which Albyn's hills
Have heard, and heard, too, have her Saxon foes: –
How in the noon of night that pibroch thrills,
Savage and shrill! But with the breath which fills   230
Their mountain-pipe, so fill the mountaineers
With the fierce native daring which instils
The stirring memory of a thousand years,
And Evan's, Donald's fame rings in each clansman's ears!

27

And Ardennes waves above them her green leaves,
Dewy with nature's tear-drops, as they pass,
Grieving, if aught inanimate e'er grieves,
Over the unreturning brave, – alas!
Ere evening to be trodden like the grass
Which now beneath them, but above shall grow   240
In its next verdure, when this fiery mass
Of living valour, rolling on the foe
And burning with high hope, shall moulder cold and low.

28

Last noon beheld them full of lusty life,
Last eve in Beauty's circle proudly gay,
The midnight brought the signal-sound of strife,
The morn the marshalling in arms, – the day
Battle's magnificently-stern array!
The thunder-clouds close o'er it, which when rent
The earth is covered thick with other clay,   250
Which her own clay shall cover, heaped and pent,
Rider and horse, – friend, foe, – in one red burial blent! [...]

36

There sunk the greatest, nor the worst of men,
Whose spirit antithetically mixt
One moment of the mightiest, and again
On little objects with like firmness fixt,
Extreme in all things! hadst thou been betwixt,   320
Thy throne had still been thine, or never been;
For daring made thy rise as fall: thou seek'st
Even now to re-assume the imperial mien,
And shake again the world, the Thunderer of the scene!

37

Conqueror and captive of the earth art thou!
She trembles at thee still, and thy wild name
Was ne'er more bruited in men's minds than now
That thou art nothing, save the jest of Fame,
Who wooed thee once, thy vassal, and became
The flatterer of thy fierceness, till thou wert   330
A god unto thyself; nor less the same
To the astounded kingdoms all inert,
Who deem'd thee for a time whate'er thou didst assert.

38

Oh, more or less than man – in high or low,
Battling with nations, flying from the field;
Now making monarchs' necks thy footstool, now
More than thy meanest soldier taught to yield;
An empire thou couldst crush, command, rebuild,
But govern not thy pettiest passion, nor,
However deeply in men's spirits skill'd,   340
Look through thine own, nor curb the lust of war,
Nor learn that tempted Fate will leave the loftiest star.

39

Yet well thy soul hath brook'd the turning tide
With that untaught innate philosophy,
Which, be it wisdom, coldness, or deep pride,
Is gall and wormwood to an enemy.
When the whole host of hatred stood hard by,
To watch and mock thee shrinking, thou hast smiled

With a sedate and all-enduring eye; –
When Fortune fled her spoil'd and favourite child,   350
He stood unbowed beneath the ills upon him piled.

40

Sager than in thy fortunes; for in them
Ambition steel'd thee on too far to show
That just habitual scorn which could contemn
Men and their thoughts; 'twas wise to feel, not so
To wear it ever on thy lip and brow,
And spurn the instruments thou wert to use
Till they were turn'd unto thine overthrow:
'Tis but a worthless world to win or lose;
So hath it proved to thee, and all such lot who choose.   360

41

If, like a tower upon a headlong rock,
Thou hadst been made to stand or fall alone,
Such scorn of man had help'd to brave the shock;
But men's thoughts were the steps which paved thy throne,
Their admiration thy best weapon shone;
The part of Philip's son was thine, not then
(Unless aside thy purple had been thrown)
Like stern Diogenes to mock at men;
For sceptred cynics earth were far too wide a den.

42

But quiet to quick bosoms is a hell,   370
And *there* hath been thy bane; there is a fire
And motion of the soul which will not dwell
In its own narrow being, but aspire
Beyond the fitting medium of desire;
And, but once kindled, quenchless evermore,
Preys upon high adventure, nor can tire
Of aught but rest; a fever at the core,
Fatal to him who bears, to all who ever bore.

43

This makes the madmen who have made men mad
By their contagion; Conquerors and Kings,   380

Founders of sects and systems, to whom add
Sophists, Bards, Statesmen, all unquiet things
Which stir too strongly the soul's secret springs,
And are themselves the fools to those they fool;
Envied, yet how unenviable! what stings
Are theirs! One breast laid open were a school
Which would unteach mankind the lust to shine or rule:

44

Their breath is agitation, and their life
A storm whereon they ride, to sink at last,
And yet so nurs'd and bigotted to strife,   390
That should their days, surviving perils past,
Melt to calm twilight, they feel overcast
With sorrow and supineness, and so die;
Even as a flame unfed, which runs to waste
With its own flickering, or a sword laid by
Which eats into itself, and rusts ingloriously.

45

He who ascends to mountain-tops, shall find
The loftiest peaks most wrapt in clouds and snow;
He who surpasses or subdues mankind,
Must look down on the hate of those below.   400
Though high *above* the sun of glory glow,
And far *beneath* the earth and ocean spread,
Round him are icy rocks, and loudly blow
Contending tempests on his naked head,
And thus reward the toils which to those summits led. [...]

67

But these are deeds which should not pass away,
And names that must not wither, though the earth
Forgets her empires with a just decay,
The enslavers and the enslaved, their death and birth;
The high, the mountain-majesty of worth
Should be, and shall, survivor of its woe,   640
And from its immortality look forth

In the sun's face, like yonder Alpine snow,
Imperishably pure beyond all things below.

68

Lake Leman woos me with its crystal face,
The mirror where the stars and mountains view
The stillness of their aspect in each trace
Its clear depth yields of their far height and hue:
There is too much of man here, to look through
With a fit mind the might which I behold;
But soon in me shall Loneliness renew   650
Thoughts hid, but not less cherish'd than of old,
Ere mingling with the herd had penn'd me in their fold.

69

To fly from, need not be to hate, mankind;
All are not fit with them to stir and toil,
Nor is it discontent to keep the mind
Deep in its fountain, lest it overboil
In the hot throng, where we become the spoil
Of our infection, till too late and long
We may deplore and struggle with the coil,   660
In wretched interchange of wrong for wrong
'Midst a contentious world, striving where none are strong.

70

There, in a moment, we may plunge our years
In fatal penitence, and in the blight
Of our own soul, turn all our blood to tears,
And colour things to come with hues of Night;
The race of life becomes a hopeless flight
To those that walk in darkness: on the sea,
The boldest steer but where their ports invite,
But there are wanderers o'er Eternity
Whose bark drives on and on, and anchored ne'er shall be.   670

71

Is it not better, then, to be alone,
And love Earth only for its earthly sake?

By the blue rushing of the arrowy Rhone,
Or the pure bosom of its nursing lake,
Which feeds it as a mother who doth make
A fair but froward infant her own care,
Kissing its cries away as these awake; –
Is it not better thus our lives to wear,
Than join the crushing crowd, doom'd to inflict or bear?

72

I live not in myself, but I become   680
Portion of that around me; and to me,
High mountains are a feeling, but the hum
Of human cities torture: I can see
Nothing to loathe in nature, save to be
A link reluctant in a fleshly chain,
Class'd among creatures, when the soul can flee,
And with the sky, the peak, the heaving plain
Of ocean, or the stars, mingle, and not in vain.

73

And thus I am absorb'd, and this is life:
I look upon the peopled desart past,   690
As on a place of agony and strife,
Where, for some sin, to Sorrow I was cast,
To act and suffer, but remount at last
With a fresh pinion; which I feel to spring,
Though young, yet waxing vigorous, as the blast
Which it would cope with, on delighted wing,
Spurning the clay-cold bonds which round our being cling.

74

And when, at length, the mind shall be all free
From what it hates in this degraded form,
Reft of its carnal life, save what shall be   700
Existent happier in the fly and worm, –
When elements to elements conform,
And dust is as it should be, shall I not
Feel all I see, less dazzling, but more warm?

The bodiless thought? the Spirit of each spot?
Of which, even now, I share at times the immortal lot?

75

Are not the mountains, waves, and skies, a part
Of me and of my soul, as I of them?
Is not the love of these deep in my heart
With a pure passion? should I not contemn   710
All objects, if compared with these? and stem
A tide of suffering, rather than forego
Such feelings for the hard and worldly phlegm
Of those whose eyes are only turn'd below,
Gazing upon the ground, with thoughts which dare not glow? [...]

85

Clear, placid Leman! thy contrasted lake,
With the wild world I dwelt in, is a thing
Which warns me, with its stillness, to forsake
Earth's troubled waters for a purer spring.   800
This quiet sail is as a noiseless wing
To waft me from distraction; once I loved
Torn ocean's roar, but thy soft murmuring
Sounds sweet as if a sister's voice reproved,
That I with stern delights should e'er have been so moved.

86

It is the hush of night, and all between
Thy margin and the mountains, dusk, yet clear,
Mellowed and mingling, yet distinctly seen,
Save darken'd Jura, whose capt heights appear
Precipitously steep; and drawing near,   810
There breathes a living fragrance from the shore,
Of flowers yet fresh with childhood; on the ear
Drops the light drip of the suspended oar,
Or chirps the grasshopper one good-night carol more;

87

He is an evening reveller, who makes
His life an infancy, and sings his fill;
At intervals, some bird from out the brakes,

Starts into voice a moment, then is still.
There seems a floating whisper on the hill,
But that is fancy, for the starlight dews   820
All silently their tears of love instil,
Weeping themselves away, till they infuse
Deep into Nature's breast the spirit of her hues.

88

Ye stars! which are the poetry of heaven!
If in your bright leaves we would read the fate
Of men and empires, – 'tis to be forgiven,
That in our aspirations to be great,
Our destinies o'erleap their mortal state,
And claim a kindred with you; for ye are
A beauty and a mystery, and create   830
In us such love and reverence from afar,
That fortune, fame, power, life, have named themselves a star.

89

All heaven and earth are still – though not in sleep,
But breathless, as we grow when feeling most;
And silent, as we stand in thoughts too deep: –
All heaven and earth are still: From the high host
Of stars, to the lull'd lake and mountain-coast,
All is concentered in a life intense,
Where not a beam, nor air, nor leaf is lost,
But hath a part of being, and a sense   840
Of that which is of all Creator and defence.

90

Then stirs the feeling infinite, so felt
In solitude, where we are *least* alone;
A truth, which through our being then doth melt
And purifies from self: it is a tone,
The soul and source of music, which makes known
Eternal harmony, and sheds a charm,
Like to the fabled Cytherea's zone,
Binding all things with beauty; – 'twould disarm
The spectre Death, had he substantial power to harm.   850

91

Not vainly did the early Persian make
His altar the high places and the peak
Of earth-o'ergazing mountains, and thus take
A fit and unwall'd temple, there to seek
The Spirit, in whose honour shrines are weak,
Uprear'd of human hands. Come, and compare
Columns and idol-dwellings, Goth or Greek,
With Nature's realms of worship, earth and air,
Nor fix on fond abodes to circumscribe thy prayer!

92

The sky is changed! – and such a change! Oh night,　　860
And storm, and darkness, ye are wondrous strong,
Yet lovely in your strength, as is the light
Of a dark eye in woman! Far along,
From peak to peak, the rattling crags among
Leaps the live thunder! Not from one lone cloud,
But every mountain now hath found a tongue,
And Jura answers, through her misty shroud,
Back to the joyous Alps, who call to her aloud!

93

And this is in the night: – Most glorious night!
Thou wert not sent for slumber! let me be　　870
A sharer in thy fierce and far delight, –
A portion of the tempest and of thee!
How the lit lake shines, a phosphoric sea,
And the big rain comes dancing to the earth!
And now again 'tis black, – and now, the glee
Of the loud hills shakes with its mountain-mirth,
As if they did rejoice o'er a young earthquake's birth.

94

Now, where the swift Rhone cleaves his way between
Heights which appear as lovers who have parted
In hate, whose mining depths so intervene,　　880
That they can meet no more, though broken-hearted;
Though in their souls, which thus each other thwarted,

Love was the very root of the fond rage
Which blighted their life's bloom, and then departed: –
Itself expired, but leaving them an age
Of years all winters, – war within themselves to wage.

95

Now, where the quick Rhone thus hath cleft his way,
The mightiest of the storms hath ta'en his stand:
For here, not one, but many, make their play,
And fling their thunder-bolts from hand to hand,   890
Flashing and cast around: of all the band,
The brightest through these parted hills hath fork'd
His lightnings, – as if he did understand,
That in such gaps as desolation work'd,
There the hot shaft should blast whatever therein lurk'd.

96

Sky, mountains, river, winds, lake, lightnings! ye!
With night, and clouds, and thunder, and a soul
To make these felt and feeling, well may be
Things that have made me watchful; the far roll
Of your departing voices, is the knoll   900
Of what in me is sleepless, – if I rest.
But where of ye, oh tempests! is the goal?
Are ye like those within the human breast?
Or do ye find, at length, like eagles, some high nest?

97

Could I embody and unbosom now
That which is most within me, – could I wreak
My thoughts upon expression, and thus throw
Soul, heart, mind, passions, feelings, strong or weak,
All that I would have sought, and all I seek,
Bear, know, feel, and yet breathe – into *one* word,   910
And that one word were Lightning, I would speak;
But as it is, I live and die unheard,
With a most voiceless thought, sheathing it as a sword. [...]

113

I have not loved the world, nor the world me;
I have not flattered its rank breath, nor bow'd   1050
To its idolatries a patient knee, –
Nor coin'd my cheek to smiles, – nor cried aloud
In worship of an echo; in the crowd
They could not deem me one of such; I stood
Among them, but not of them; in a shroud
Of thoughts which were not their thoughts, and still could,
Had I not filed my mind, which thus itself subdued.

114

I have not loved the world, nor the world me, –
But let us part fair foes; I do believe,
Though I have found them not, that there may be   1060
Words which are things, – hopes which will not deceive,
And virtues which are merciful, nor weave
Snares for the failing: I would also deem
O'er others' griefs that some sincerely grieve;
That two, or one, are almost what they seem, –
That goodness is no name, and happiness no dream.

115

My daughter! with thy name this song begun –
My daughter! with thy name thus much shall end –
I see thee not, – I hear thee not, – but none
Can be so wrapt in thee; thou art the friend   1070
To whom the shadows of far years extend:
Albeit my brow thou never should'st behold,
My voice shall with thy future visions blend,
And reach into thy heart, – when mine is cold, –
A token and a tone, even from thy father's mould.

116

To aid thy mind's development, – to watch
Thy dawn of little joys, – to sit and see
Almost thy very growth, – to view thee catch
Knowledge of objects, – wonders yet to thee!
To hold thee lightly on a gentle knee,   1080

And print on thy soft cheek a parent's kiss, –
This, it should seem, was not reserv'd for me;
Yet this was in my nature: – as it is,
I know not what is there, yet something like to this.

117

Yet, though dull Hate as duty should be taught,
I know that thou wilt love me; though my name
Should be shut from thee, as a spell still fraught
With desolation, – and a broken claim:
Though the grave closed between us, – 'twere the same,
I know that thou wilt love me; though to drain   1090
My blood from out thy being, were an aim,
And an attainment, – all would be in vain, –
Still thou would'st love me, still that more than life retain.

118

The child of love, – though born in bitterness,
And nurtured in convulsion, – of thy sire
These were the elements, – and thine no less.
As yet such are around thee, – but thy fire
Shall be more tempered, and thy hope far higher.
Sweet be thy cradled slumbers! O'er the sea,
And from the mountains where I now respire,   1100
Fain would I waft such blessing upon thee,
As, with a sigh, I deem thou might'st have been to me!

Sonnet on Chillon

Eternal spirit of the chainless mind!
    Brightest in dungeons, Liberty! thou art,
    For there thy habitation is the heart –
The heart which love of thee alone can bind;
And when thy sons to fetters are consigned –
    To fetters, and the damp vault's dayless gloom,

Their country conquers with their martyrdom,
And Freedom's fame finds wings on every wind.

Chillon! thy prison is a holy place,
    And thy sad floor an altar – for 'twas trod,   10
Until his very steps have left a trace
    Worn, as if thy cold pavement were a sod,
By Bonnivard! – May none those marks efface!
    For they appeal from tyranny to God.

[Epistle to Augusta]

1

My Sister – my sweet Sister – if a name
    Dearer and purer were – it should be thine.
Mountains and Seas divide us – but I claim
    No tears – but tenderness to answer mine:
Go where I will, to me thou art the same –
    A loved regret which I would not resign –
There yet are two things in my destiny
A world to roam through – and a home with thee.

2

The first were nothing – had I still the last
    It were the haven of my happiness –   10
But other claims and other ties thou hast –
    And mine is not the wish to make them less.
A strange doom was thy father's son's and past
    Recalling – as it lies beyond redress –
Reversed for him our grandsire's fate of yore
He had no rest at sea – nor I on shore.

3

If my inheritance of storms hath been
    In other elements – and on the rocks
Of perils overlooked or unforeseen
    I have sustained my share of worldly shocks   20

The fault was mine – nor do I seek to screen
    My errors with defensive paradox –
I have been cunning in mine overthrow
The careful pilot of my proper woe.

                            4

Mine were my faults – and mine be their reward –
    My whole life was a contest – since the day
That gave me being gave me that which marred
    The gift – a fate or will that walked astray –
And I at times have found the struggle hard
    And thought of shaking off my bonds of clay –   30
But now I fain would for a time survive
If but to see what next can well arrive.

                            5

Kingdoms and empires in my little day
    I have outlived and yet I am not old –
And when I look on this, the petty spray
    Of my own years of trouble, which have rolled
Like a wild bay of breakers, melts away: –
    Something – I know not what – does still uphold
A spirit of slight patience; – not in vain
Even for its own sake – do we purchase pain.   40

                            6

Perhaps – the workings of defiance stir
    Within me, – or perhaps a cold despair –
Brought on when ills habitually recur, –
    Perhaps a harder clime – or purer air –
For to all such may change of soul refer –
    And with light armour we may learn to bear –
Have taught me a strange quiet which was not
The chief companion of a calmer lot.

                            7

I feel almost at times as I have felt
    In happy childhood – trees and flowers and brooks   50
Which do remember me of where I dwelt
    Ere my young mind was sacrificed to books –

Come as of yore upon me – and can melt
  My heart with recognition of their looks –
And even at moments I could think I see
Some living things to love – but none like thee.

8

Here are the Alpine landscapes – which create
  A fund for contemplation – to admire
Is a brief feeling of a trivial date –
  But something worthier do such scenes inspire: 60
Here to be lonely is not desolate –
  For much I view which I could most desire –
And above all a lake I can behold –
Lovelier – not dearer – than our own of old.

9

Oh that thou wert but with me! – but I grow
  The fool of my own wishes – and forget
The solitude which I have vaunted so
  Has lost its praise in this but one regret –
There may be others which I less may show –
  I am not of the plaintive mood – and yet   70
I feel an ebb in my philosophy
And the tide rising in my altered eye.

10

I did remind thee of our own dear lake
  By the old Hall which may be mine no more –
Leman's is fair – but think not I forsake
  The sweet remembrance of a dearer shore –
Sad havoc Time must with my memory make
  Ere *that* or *thou* can fade these eyes before –
Though like all things which I have loved – they are
Resigned for ever – or divided far.   80

11

The world is all before me – I but ask
  Of Nature that with which she will comply –
It is but in her Summer's sun to bask –
  To mingle in the quiet of her sky –

To see her gentle face without a mask
   And never gaze on it with apathy –
She was my early friend – and now shall be
My Sister – till I look again on thee.

12

I can reduce all feelings but this one
   And that I would not – for at length I see   90
Such scenes as those wherein my life begun
   The earliest – were the only paths for me.
Had I but sooner known the crowd to shun
   I had been better than I now can be
The passions which have torn me would have slept –
I had not suffered – and *thou* hadst not wept.

13

With false Ambition what had I to do?
   Little with love, and least of all with fame!
And yet they came unsought and with me grew,
   And made me all which they can make – a Name.   100
Yet this was not the end I did pursue –
   Surely I once beheld a nobler aim.
But all is over – I am one the more
To baffled millions which have gone before.

14

And for the future – this world's future may
   From me demand but little from my care;
I have outlived myself by many a day,
   Having survived so many things that were –
My years have been no slumber – but the prey
   Of ceaseless vigils; – for I had the share   110
Of life which might have filled a century
Before its fourth in time had passed me by.

15

And for the remnants which may be to come
   I am content – and for the past I feel
Not thankless – for within the crowded sum
   Of struggles – happiness at times would steal

And for the present – I would not benumb
   My feelings farther – nor shall I conceal
That with all this I still can look around
And worship Nature with a thought profound.   120

16

For thee – my own sweet Sister – in thy heart
   I know myself secure – as thou in mine
We were and are – I am – even as thou art –
   Beings – who ne'er each other can resign
It is the same together or apart –
   From life's commencement to its slow decline –
We are entwined – let death come slow or fast
The tie which bound the first endures the last.

Darkness

I had a dream, which was not all a dream.
The bright sun was extinguish'd, and the stars
Did wander darkling in the eternal space,
Rayless, and pathless, and the icy earth
Swung blind and blackening in the moonless air;
Morn came, and went – and came, and brought no day,
And men forgot their passions in the dread
Of this their desolation; and all hearts
Were chill'd into a selfish prayer for light:
And they did live by watchfires – and the thrones,   10
The palaces of crowned kings – the huts,
The habitations of all things which dwell,
Were burnt for beacons; cities were consumed,
And men were gathered round their blazing homes
To look once more into each other's face;
Happy were those who dwelt within the eye
Of the volcanos, and their mountain-torch:
A fearful hope was all the world contain'd;
Forests were set on fire – but hour by hour

They fell and faded – and the crackling trunks   20
Extinguish'd with a crash – and all was black.
The brows of men by the despairing light
Wore an unearthly aspect, as by fits
The flashes fell upon them; some lay down
And hid their eyes and wept; and some did rest
Their chins upon their clenched hands, and smiled;
And others hurried to and fro, and fed
Their funeral piles with fuel, and looked up
With mad disquietude on the dull sky,
The pall of a past world; and then again   30
With curses cast them down upon the dust,
And gnash'd their teeth and howl'd: the wild birds shriek'd,
And, terrified, did flutter on the ground,
And flap their useless wings; the wildest brutes
Came tame and tremulous; and vipers crawl'd
And twined themselves among the multitude,
Hissing, but stingless – they were slain for food:
And War, which for a moment was no more,
Did glut himself again; – a meal was bought
With blood, and each sate sullenly apart   40
Gorging himself in gloom: no love was left;
All earth was but one thought – and that was death,
Immediate and inglorious; and the pang
Of famine fed upon all entrails – men
Died, and their bones were tombless as their flesh;
The meagre by the meagre were devoured,
Even dogs assail'd their masters, all save one,
And he was faithful to a corse, and kept
The birds and beasts and famish'd men at bay,
Till hunger clung them, or the dropping dead   50
Lured their lank jaws; himself sought out no food,
But with a piteous and perpetual moan
And a quick desolate cry, licking the hand
Which answered not with a caress – he died.
The crowd was famish'd by degrees; but two
Of an enormous city did survive,
And they were enemies; they met beside
The dying embers of an altar-place
Where had been heap'd a mass of holy things

For an unholy usage; they raked up,   60
And shivering scraped with their cold skeleton hands
The feeble ashes, and their feeble breath
Blew for a little life, and made a flame
Which was a mockery; then they lifted up
Their eyes as it grew lighter, and beheld
Each other's aspects – saw, and shriek'd, and died –
Even of their mutual hideousness they died,
Unknowing who he was upon whose brow
Famine had written Fiend. The world was void,
The populous and the powerful – was a lump,   70
Seasonless, herbless, treeless, manless, lifeless –
A lump of death – a chaos of hard clay.
The rivers, lakes, and ocean all stood still,
And nothing stirred within their silent depths;
Ships sailorless lay rotting on the sea,
And their masts fell down piecemeal; as they dropp'd
They slept on the abyss without a surge –
The waves were dead; the tides were in their grave,
The moon their mistress had expired before;
The winds were withered in the stagnant air,   80
And the clouds perish'd; Darkness had no need
Of aid from them – She was the universe.

from Childe Harold's Pilgrimage
Canto IV

1

I stood in Venice, on the Bridge of Sighs;
A palace and a prison on each hand:
I saw from out the wave her structures rise
As from the stroke of the enchanter's wand:
A thousand years their cloudy wings expand
Around me, and a dying Glory smiles
O'er the far times, when many a subject land

Look'd to the winged Lion's marble piles,
Where Venice sate in state, thron'd on her hundred isles!

2

She looks a sea Cybele, fresh from ocean,   10
Rising with her tiara of proud towers
At airy distance, with majestic motion,
A ruler of the waters and their powers:
And such she was; – her daughters had their dowers
From spoils of nations, and the exhaustless East
Pour'd in her lap all gems in sparkling showers.
In purple was she robed, and of her feast
Monarchs partook, and deem'd their dignity increas'd.

3

In Venice Tasso's echoes are no more,
And silent rows the songless gondolier;   20
Her palaces are crumbling to the shore,
And music meets not always now the ear:
Those days are gone – but Beauty still is here.
States fall, arts fade – but Nature doth not die,
Nor yet forget how Venice once was dear,
The pleasant place of all festivity,
The revel of the earth, the masque of Italy!

4

But unto us she hath a spell beyond
Her name in story, and her long array
Of mighty shadows, whose dim forms despond   30
Above the dogeless city's vanish'd sway;
Ours is a trophy which will not decay
With the Rialto; Shylock and the Moor,
And Pierre, can not be swept or worn away –
The keystones of the arch! though all were o'er,
For us repeopled were the solitary shore.

5

The beings of the mind are not of clay;
Essentially immortal, they create
And multiply in us a brighter ray

And more beloved existence: that which Fate   40
Prohibits to dull life, in this our state
Of mortal bondage, by these spirits supplied
First exiles, then replaces what we hate;
Watering the heart whose early flowers have died,
And with a fresher growth replenishing the void.

6

Such is the refuge of our youth and age,
The first from Hope, the last from Vacancy;
And this worn feeling peoples many a page,
And, may be, that which grows beneath mine eye:
Yet there are things whose strong reality   50
Outshines our fairy-land; in shape and hues
More beautiful than our fantastic sky,
And the strange constellations which the Muse
O'er her wild universe is skilful to diffuse:

7

I saw or dreamed of such, – but let them go –
They came like truth, and disappeared like dreams;
And whatsoe'er they were – are now but so:
I could replace them if I would, still teems
My mind with many a form which aptly seems
Such as I sought for, and at moments found;   60
Let these too go – for waking Reason deems
Such over-weening phantasies unsound,
And other voices speak, and other sights surround. [...]

139

And here the buzz of eager nations ran,
In murmured pity, or loud-roared applause,
As man was slaughtered by his fellow man.
And wherefore slaughtered? wherefore, but because
Such were the bloody Circus' genial laws,
And the imperial pleasure. – Wherefore not?
What matters where we fall to fill the maws
Of worms – on battle-plains or listed spot?   1250
Both are but theatres where the chief actors rot.

140

I see before me the Gladiator lie:
He leans upon his hand – his manly brow
Consents to death, but conquers agony,
And his drooped head sinks gradually low –
And through his side the last drops, ebbing slow
From the red gash, fall heavy, one by one,
Like the first of a thunder-shower; and now
The arena swims around him – he is gone,
Ere ceased the inhuman shout which hail'd the wretch who
  won.   1260

141

He heard it, but he heeded not – his eyes
Were with his heart, and that was far away;
He reck'd not of the life he lost nor prize,
But where his rude hut by the Danube lay
There were his young barbarians all at play,
There was their Dacian mother – he, their sire,
Butcher'd to make a Roman holiday –
All this rush'd with his blood – Shall he expire
And unavenged? – Arise! ye Goths, and glut your ire!

142

But here, where Murder breathed her bloody stream;   1270
And here, where buzzing nations choked the ways,
And roar'd or murmur'd like a mountain stream
Dashing or winding as its torrent strays;
Here, where the Roman million's blame or praise
Was death or life, the playthings of a crowd,
My voice sounds much – and fall the stars' faint rays
On the arena void – seats crush'd – walls bow'd –
And galleries, where my steps seem echoes strangely loud.

143

A ruin – yet what ruin! from its mass
Walls, palaces, half-cities, have been reared;   1280
Yet oft the enormous skeleton ye pass
And marvel where the spoil could have appeared.
Hath it indeed been plundered, or but cleared?

Alas! developed, opens the decay,
When the colossal fabric's form is neared:
It will not bear the brightness of the day,
Which streams too much on all years, man, have reft away.

144

But when the rising moon begins to climb
Its topmost arch, and gently pauses there;
When the stars twinkle through the loops of time,   1290
And the low night-breeze waves along the air
The garland-forest, which the grey walls wear,
Like laurels on the bald first Caesar's head;
When the light shines serene but doth not glare,
Then in this magic circle raise the dead:
Heroes have trod this spot – 'tis on their dust ye tread.

145

'While stands the Coliseum, Rome shall stand;
When falls the Coliseum, Rome shall fall;
And when Rome falls – the World.' From our own land
Thus spake the pilgrims o'er this mighty wall   1300
In Saxon times, which we are wont to call
Ancient; and these three mortal things are still
On their foundations, and unaltered all;
Rome and her Ruin past Redemption's skill,
The World, the same wide den – of thieves, or what ye will. [...]

154

But thou, of temples old, or altars new,
Standest alone – with nothing like to thee –
Worthiest of God, the holy and the true.   1380
Since Zion's desolation, when that He
Forsook his former city, what could be,
Of earthly structures, in his honour piled,
Of a sublimer aspect? Majesty,
Power, Glory, Strength, and Beauty, all are aisled
In this eternal ark of worship undefiled.

155

Enter: its grandeur overwhelms thee not;
And why? it is not lessened; but thy mind,

Expanded by the genius of the spot,
Has grown colossal, and can only find   1390
A fit abode wherein appear enshrined
Thy hopes of immortality; and thou
Shalt one day, if found worthy, so defined,
See thy God face to face, as thou dost now
His Holy of Holies, nor be blasted by his brow.

156

Thou movest – but increasing with the advance,
Like climbing some great Alp, which still doth rise,
Deceived by its gigantic elegance;
Vastness which grows – but grows to harmonize –
All musical in its immensities;   1400
Rich marbles – richer painting – shrines where flame
The lamps of gold – and haughty dome which vies
In air with Earth's chief structures, though their frame
Sits on the firm-set ground – and this the clouds must claim.

157

Thou seest not all; but piecemeal thou must break,
To separate contemplation, the great whole;
And as the ocean many bays will make,
That ask the eye – so here condense thy soul
To more immediate objects, and control
Thy thoughts until thy mind hath got by heart   1410
Its eloquent proportions, and unroll
In mighty graduations, part by part,
The glory which at once upon thee did not dart,

158

Not by its fault – but thine: Our outward sense
Is but of gradual grasp – and as it is
That what we have of feeling most intense
Outstrips our faint expression; even so this
Outshining and o'erwhelming edifice
Fools our fond gaze, and greatest of the great
Defies at first our Nature's littleness,   1420
Till, growing with its growth, we thus dilate
Our spirits to the size of that they contemplate.

159

Then pause, and be enlightened; there is more
In such a survey than the sating gaze
Of wonder pleased, or awe which would adore
The worship of the place, or the mere praise
Of art and its great masters, who could raise
What former time, nor skill, nor thought could plan;
The fountain of sublimity displays
Its depth, and thence may draw the mind of man   1430
Its golden sands, and learn what great conceptions can.

160

Or, turning to the Vatican, go see
Laocoon's torture dignifying pain –
A father's love and mortal's agony
With an immortal's patience blending:– Vain
The struggle; vain, against the coiling strain
And gripe, and deepening of the dragon's grasp,
The old man's clench; the long envenomed chain
Rivets the living links, – the enormous asp   1440
Enforces pang on pang, and stifles gasp on gasp.

161

Or view the Lord of the unerring bow,
The God of life, and poesy, and light –
The Sun in human limbs arrayed, and brow
All radiant from his triumph in the fight;
The shaft hath just been shot – the arrow bright
With an immortal's vengeance; in his eye
And nostril beautiful disdain, and might,
And majesty, flash their full lightnings by,
Developing in that one glance the Deity.

162

But in his delicate form – a dream of Love,   1450
Shaped by some solitary nymph, whose breast
Long'd for a deathless lover from above,
And madden'd in that vision – are exprest
All that ideal beauty ever bless'd

The mind within its most unearthly mood,
When each conception was a heavenly guest –
A ray of immortality – and stood,
Starlike, around, until they gathered to a god!

163

And if it be Prometheus stole from Heaven
The fire which we endure, it was repaid   1460
By him to whom the energy was given
Which this poetic marble hath array'd
With an eternal glory – which, if made
By human hands, is not of human thought;
And Time himself hath hallowed it, nor laid
One ringlet in the dust – nor hath it caught
A tinge of years, but breathes the flame with which 'twas
    wrought. [...]

178

There is a pleasure in the pathless woods,
There is a rapture on the lonely shore,
There is society, where none intrudes,
By the deep Sea, and music in its roar:
I love not Man the less, but Nature more,
From these our interviews, in which I steal
From all I may be, or have been before,   1600
To mingle with the Universe, and feel
What I can ne'er express, yet can not all conceal.

179

Roll on, thou deep and dark blue ocean – roll!
Ten thousand fleets sweep over thee in vain;
Man marks the earth with ruin – his control
Stops with the shore; – upon the watery plain
The wrecks are all thy deed, nor doth remain
A shadow of man's ravage, save his own,
When, for a moment, like a drop of rain,
He sinks into thy depths with bubbling groan,   1610
Without a grave, unknell'd, uncoffin'd, and unknown.

180

His steps are not upon thy paths, – thy fields
Are not a spoil for him, – thou dost arise
And shake him from thee; the vile strength he wields
For earth's destruction thou dost all despise,
Spurning him from thy bosom to the skies,
And send'st him, shivering in thy playful spray
And howling, to his Gods, where haply lies
His petty hope in some near port or bay,
And dashest him again to earth: – there let him lay.   1620

181

The armaments which thunderstrike the walls
Of rock-built cities, bidding nations quake,
And monarchs tremble in their capitals,
The oak leviathans, whose huge ribs make
Their clay creator the vain title take
Of lord of thee, and arbiter of war;
These are thy toys, and, as the snowy flake,
They melt into thy yeast of waves, which mar
Alike the Armada's pride, or spoils of Trafalgar.

182

Thy shores are empires, changed in all save thee –   1630
Assyria, Greece, Rome, Carthage, what are they?
Thy waters washed them power while they were free,
And many a tyrant since; their shores obey
The stranger, slave, or savage; their decay
Has dried up realms to desarts: – not so thou,
Unchangeable save to thy wild waves' play –
Time writes no wrinkle on thine azure brow –
Such as creation's dawn beheld, thou rollest now.

183

Thou glorious mirror, where the Almighty's form
Glasses itself in tempests; in all time,   1640
Calm or convuls'd – in breeze, or gale, or storm,
Icing the pole, or in the torrid clime
Dark-heaving; – boundless, endless, and sublime –

The image of Eternity – the throne
Of the Invisible; even from out thy slime
The monsters of the deep are made; each zone
Obeys thee; thou goest forth, dread, fathomless, alone.

184

And I have loved thee, Ocean! and my joy
Of youthful sports was on thy breast to be
Borne, like thy bubbles, onward: from a boy   1650
I wantoned with thy breakers – they to me
Were a delight; and if the freshening sea
Made them a terror – 'twas a pleasing fear,
For I was as it were a child of thee,
And trusted to thy billows far and near,
And laid my hand upon thy mane – as I do here.

185

My task is done – my song hath ceased – my theme
Has died into an echo; it is fit
The spell should break of this protracted dream.
The torch shall be extinguish'd which hath lit   1660
My midnight lamp – and what is writ, is writ, –
Would it were worthier! but I am not now
That which I have been – and my visions flit
Less palpably before me – and the glow
Which in my spirit dwelt, is fluttering, faint, and low.

186

Farewell! a word that must be, and hath been –
A sound which makes us linger; – yet – farewell!
Ye! who have traced the Pilgrim to the scene
Which is his last, if in your memories dwell
A thought which once was his, if on ye swell   1670
A single recollection, not in vain
He wore his sandal-shoon, and scallop-shell;
Farewell! with *him* alone may rest the pain,
If such there were – with *you*, the moral of his strain!

['So, We'll Go No More A Roving']

1

So, we'll go no more a roving
   So late into the night,
Though the heart be still as loving,
   And the moon be still as bright.

2

For the sword outwears its sheath,
   And the soul wears out the breast,
And the heart must pause to breathe,
   And love itself have rest.

3

Though the night was made for loving,
   And the day returns too soon,   10
Yet we'll go no more a roving
   By the light of the moon.

from Beppo, A Venetian Story

41

With all its sinful doings, I must say,
   That Italy's a pleasant place to me,
Who love to see the Sun shine every day,
   And vines (not nail'd to walls) from tree to tree
Festoon'd, much like the back scene of a play,
   Or melodrame, which people flock to see,
When the first act is ended by a dance,
In vineyards copied from the south of France.

42

I like on Autumn evenings to ride out,
   Without being forc'd to bid my groom be sure   330

My cloak is round his middle strapp'd about,
　　Because the skies are not the most secure;
I know too that, if stopp'd upon my route,
　　Where the green alleys windingly allure,
Reeling with *grapes* red waggons choke the way, –
In England 'twould be dung, dust, or a dray.

43

I also like to dine on becaficas,
　　To see the Sun set, sure he'll rise to-morrow,
Not through a misty morning twinkling weak as
　　A drunken man's dead eye in maudlin sorrow,
But with all Heaven t' himself; that day will break as
　　Beauteous as cloudless, nor be forc'd to borrow
That sort of farthing candlelight which glimmers
Where reeking London's smoky cauldron simmers.

340

44

I love the language, that soft bastard Latin,
　　Which melts like kisses from a female mouth,
And sounds as if it should be writ on satin,
　　With syllables which breathe of the sweet South,
And gentle liquids gliding all so pat in,
　　That not a single accent seems uncouth,
Like our harsh northern whistling, grunting guttural,
Which we're oblig'd to hiss, and spit, and sputter all.

350

45

I like the women too (forgive my folly),
　　From the rich peasant-cheek of ruddy bronze,
And large black eyes that flash on you a volley
　　Of rays that say a thousand things at once,
To the high dama's brow, more melancholy,
　　But clear, and with a wild and liquid glance,
Heart on her lips, and soul within her eyes,
Soft as her clime, and sunny as her skies.

360

46

Eve of the land which still is Paradise!
   Italian beauty! didst thou not inspire
Raphael, who died in thy embrace, and vies
   With all we know of Heaven, or can desire,
In what he hath bequeath'd us? – in what guise,
   Though flashing from the fervour of the lyre,
Would *words* describe thy past and present glow,
While yet Canova can create below?

47

'England! with all thy faults I love thee still,'
   I said at Calais, and have not forgot it;   370
I like to speak and lucubrate my fill;
   I like the government (but that is not it);
I like the freedom of the press and quill;
   I like the Habeas Corpus (when we've got it);
I like a parliamentary debate,
Particularly when 'tis not too late;

48

I like the taxes when they're not too many;
   I like a seacoal fire, when not too dear;
I like a beef-steak, too, as well as any;
   Have no objection to a pot of beer;   380
I like the weather, when it is not rainy,

Note to Stanza 46

(In talking thus, the writer, more especially
   Of women, would be understood to say,
He speaks as a spectator, not officially,
   And always, reader, in a modest way;
Perhaps, too, in no very great degree shall he
   Appear to have offended in this lay,
Since, as all know, without the sex, our sonnets
Would seem unfinish'd, like their untrimm'd bonnets.)

That is, I like two months of every year.
And so God save the Regent, Church, and King!
Which means that I like all and every thing.

49

Our standing army, and disbanded seamen,
   Poor's rate, Reform, my own, the nation's debt,
Our little riots just to show we are free men,
   Our trifling bankruptcies in the Gazette,
Our cloudy climate, and our chilly women,
   All these I can forgive, and those forget,   390
And greatly venerate our recent glories,
And wish they were not owing to the Tories.

from **Don Juan Canto I**

[Juan's first love]

90

Young Juan wander'd by the glassy brooks
   Thinking unutterable things; he threw
Himself at length within the leafy nooks
   Where the wild branch of the cork forest grew;
There poets find materials for their books,
   And every now and then we read them through,
So that their plan and prosody are eligible,
Unless, like Wordsworth, they prove unintelligible.   720

91

He, Juan (and not Wordsworth), so pursued
   His self-communion with his own high soul,
Until his mighty heart, in its great mood,
   Had mitigated part, though not the whole
Of its disease; he did the best he could
   With things not very subject to control,

And turn'd, without perceiving his condition,
Like Coleridge, into a metaphysician.

92
He thought about himself, and the whole earth,
   Of man the wonderful, and of the stars,   730
And how the deuce they ever could have birth;
   And then he thought of earthquakes, and of wars,
How many miles the moon might have in girth,
   Of air-balloons, and of the many bars
To perfect knowledge of the boundless skies;
And then he thought of Donna Julia's eyes.

93
In thoughts like these true wisdom may discern
   Longings sublime, and aspirations high,
Which some are born with, but the most part learn
   To plague themselves withal, they know not why: 740
'Twas strange that one so young should thus concern
   His brain about the action of the sky;
If *you* think 'twas philosophy that this did,
I can't help thinking puberty assisted.

94
He pored upon the leaves, and on the flowers,
   And heard a voice in all the winds; and then
He thought of wood nymphs and immortal bowers,
   And how the goddesses came down to men:
He miss'd the pathway, he forgot the hours,
   And when he look'd upon his watch again,   750
He found how much old Time had been a winner –
He also found that he had lost his dinner.

95
Sometimes he turn'd to gaze upon his book,
   Boscan, or Garcilasso; – by the wind
Even as the page is rustled while we look,
   So by the poesy of his own mind
Over the mystic leaf his soul was shook,
   As if 'twere one whereon magicians bind

Their spells, and give them to the passing gale,
According to some good old woman's tale.   760

96

Thus would he while his lonely hours away
  Dissatisfied, nor knowing what he wanted;
Nor glowing reverie, nor poet's lay,
  Could yield his spirit that for which it panted,
A bosom whereon he his head might lay,
  And hear the heart beat with the love it granted,
With — several other things, which I forget,
Or which, at least, I need not mention yet.

97

Those lonely walks, and lengthening reveries,
  Could not escape the gentle Julia's eyes;   770
She saw that Juan was not at his ease;
  But that which chiefly may, and must surprise,
Is, that the Donna Inez did not tease
  Her only son with question or surmise;
Whether it was she did not see, or would not,
Or, like all very clever people, could not.

98

This may seem strange, but yet 'tis very common;
  For instance – gentlemen, whose ladies take
Leave to o'erstep the written rights of woman,
  And break the — Which commandment is't they break?   780
(I have forgot the number, and think no man
  Should rashly quote, for fear of a mistake.)
I say, when these same gentlemen are jealous,
They make some blunder, which their ladies tell us.

99

A real husband always is suspicious,
  But still no less suspects in the wrong place,
Jealous of some one who had no such wishes,
  Or pandering blindly to his own disgrace
By harbouring some dear friend extremely vicious;

The last indeed's infallibly the case: 790
And when the spouse and friend are gone off wholly,
He wonders at their vice, and not his folly.

100

Thus parents also are at times short-sighted;
   Though watchful as the lynx, they ne'er discover,
The while the wicked world beholds delighted,
   Young Hopeful's mistress, or Miss Fanny's lover,
Till some confounded escapade has blighted
   The plan of twenty years, and all is over;
And then the mother cries, the father swears,
And wonders why the devil he got heirs.   800

101

But Inez was so anxious, and so clear
   Of sight, that I must think, on this occasion,
She had some other motive much more near
   For leaving Juan to this new temptation;
But what that motive was, I sha'n't say here;
   Perhaps to finish Juan's education,
Perhaps to open Don Alfonso's eyes,
In case he thought his wife too great a prize.

102

It was upon a day, a summer's day; –
   Summer's indeed a very dangerous season,   810
And so is spring about the end of May;
   The sun, no doubt, is the prevailing reason;
But whatsoe'er the cause is, one may say,
   And stand convicted of more truth than treason,
That there are months which nature grows more merry in,
March has its hares, and May must have its heroine.

103

'Twas on a summer's day – the sixth of June: –
   I like to be particular in dates,
Not only of the age, and year, but moon;
   They are a sort of post-house, where the Fates   820

Change horses, making history change its tune,
    Then spur away o'er empires and o'er states,
Leaving at last not much besides chronology,
Excepting the post-obits of theology.

104

'Twas on the sixth of June, about the hour
    Of half-past six – perhaps still nearer seven,
When Julia sate within as pretty a bower
    As e'er held houri in that heathenish heaven
Described by Mahomet, and Anacreon Moore,
    To whom the lyre and laurels have been given,   830
With all the trophies of triumphant song –
He won them well, and may he wear them long!

105

She sate, but not alone; I know not well
    How this same interview had taken place,
And even if I knew, I should not tell –
    People should hold their tongues in any case;
No matter how or why the thing befell,
    But there were she and Juan, face to face –
When two such faces are so, 'twould be wise,
But very difficult, to shut their eyes.   840

106

How beautiful she look'd! her conscious heart
    Glow'd in her cheek, and yet she felt no wrong.
Oh Love! how perfect is thy mystic art,
    Strengthening the weak, and trampling on the strong,
How self-deceitful is the sagest part
    Of mortals whom thy lure hath led along –
The precipice she stood on was immense,
So was her creed in her own innocence.

107

She thought of her own strength, and Juan's youth,
    And of the folly of all prudish fears,   850
Victorious virtue, and domestic truth,

And then of Don Alfonso's fifty years:
I wish these last had not occurr'd, in sooth,
    Because that number rarely much endears,
And through all climes, the snowy and the sunny,
Sounds ill in love, whate'er it may in money.

108

When people say, 'I've told you *fifty* times,'
    They mean to scold, and very often do;
When poets say, 'I've written *fifty* rhymes,'
    They make you dread that they'll recite them too;   860
In gangs of *fifty*, thieves commit their crimes;
    At *fifty* love for love is rare, 'tis true,
But then, no doubt, it equally as true is,
A good deal may be bought for *fifty* Louis.

109

Julia had honour, virtue, truth, and love,
    For Don Alfonso; and she inly swore,
By all the vows below to powers above,
    She never would disgrace the ring she wore,
Nor leave a wish which wisdom might reprove;
    And while she ponder'd this, besides much more,   870
One hand on Juan's carelessly was thrown,
Quite by mistake – she thought it was her own;

110

Unconsciously she lean'd upon the other,
    Which play'd within the tangles of her hair;
And to contend with thoughts she could not smother,
    She seem'd by the distraction of her air.
'Twas surely very wrong in Juan's mother
    To leave together this imprudent pair,
She who for many years had watch'd her son so –
I'm very certain *mine* would not have done so.   880

111

The hand which still held Juan's, by degrees
    Gently, but palpably confirm'd its grasp,

As if it said 'detain me, if you please;'
   Yet there's no doubt she only meant to clasp
His fingers with a pure Platonic squeeze;
   She would have shrunk as from a toad, or asp,
Had she imagined such a thing could rouse
A feeling dangerous to a prudent spouse.

112

I cannot know what Juan thought of this,
   But what he did, is much what you would do;   890
His young lip thank'd it with a grateful kiss,
   And then, abash'd at its own joy, withdrew
In deep despair, lest he had done amiss,
   Love is so very timid when 'tis new:
She blush'd, and frown'd not, but she strove to speak,
And held her tongue, her voice was grown so weak.

113

The sun set, and up rose the yellow moon:
   The devil's in the moon for mischief; they
Who call'd her CHASTE, methinks, began too soon
   Their nomenclature, there is not a day,   900
The longest, not the twenty-first of June,
   Sees half the business in a wicked way
On which three single hours of moonshine smile –
And then she looks so modest all the while.

114

There is a dangerous silence in that hour,
   A stillness, which leaves room for the full soul
To open all itself, without the power
   Of calling wholly back its self-control;
The silver light which, hallowing tree and tower,
   Sheds beauty and deep softness o'er the whole,   910
Breathes also to the heart, and o'er it throws
A loving languor, which is not repose.

115

And Julia sate with Juan, half embraced
   And half retiring from the glowing arm,

Which trembled like the bosom where 'twas placed;
   Yet still she must have thought there was no harm,
Or else 'twere easy to withdraw her waist;
   But then the situation had its charm,
And then – God knows what next – I can't go on;
I'm almost sorry that I e'er begun.   920

from Don Juan Canto II

[The affair discovered, Juan is sent abroad]

14

Don Juan stood, and, gazing from the stern,
   Beheld his native Spain receding far:
First partings form a lesson hard to learn,
   Even nations feel this when they go to war;
There is a sort of unexprest concern,
   A kind of shock that sets one's heart ajar: 110
At leaving even the most unpleasant people
And places, one keeps looking at the steeple.

15

But Juan had got many things to leave,
   His mother, and a mistress, and no wife,
So that he had much better cause to grieve
   Than many persons more advanced in life;
And if we now and then a sigh must heave
   At quitting even those we quit in strife,
No doubt we weep for those the heart endears –
That is, till deeper griefs congeal our tears.   120

16

So Juan wept, as wept the captive Jews
   By Babel's waters, still remembering Sion:
I'd weep, but mine is not a weeping Muse,
   And such light griefs are not a thing to die on;

Young men should travel, if but to amuse
    Themselves; and the next time their servants tie on
Behind their carriages their new portmanteau,
Perhaps it may be lined with this my canto.

17

And Juan wept, and much he sigh'd and thought,
    While his salt tears dropp'd into the salt sea,   130
'Sweets to the sweet;' (I like so much to quote;
    You must excuse this extract, 'tis where she,
The Queen of Denmark, for Ophelia brought
    Flowers to the grave); and sobbing often, he
Reflected on his present situation,
And seriously resolved on reformation.

18

'Farewell, my Spain! a long farewell!' he cried,
    'Perhaps I may revisit thee no more,
But die, as many an exiled heart hath died,
    Of its own thirst to see again thy shore: 140
Farewell, where Guadalquivir's waters glide!
    Farewell, my mother! and, since all is o'er,
Farewell, too dearest Julia!, – (here he drew
Her letter out again, and read it through.)

19

'And oh! if e'er I should forget, I swear –
    But that's impossible, and cannot be –
Sooner shall this blue ocean melt to air,
    Sooner shall earth resolve itself to sea,
Than I resign thine image, Oh! my fair!
    Or think of any thing excepting thee;   150
A mind diseased no remedy can physic –'
(Here the ship gave a lurch, and he grew sea-sick.)

20

'Sooner shall heaven kiss earth' – (here he fell sicker)
    'Oh, Julia! what is every other woe? –
(For God's sake let me have a glass of liquor,
    Pedro, Battista, help me down below.)

Julia, my love! – (you rascal, Pedro, quicker) –
    Oh Julia! – (this curst vessel pitches so) –
Beloved Julia, hear me still beseeching!'
(Here he grew inarticulate with reaching.)   160

21

He felt that chilling heaviness of heart,
    Or rather stomach, which, alas! attends,
Beyond the best apothecary's art,
    The loss of love, the treachery of friends,
Or death of those we doat on, when a part
    Of us dies with them as each fond hope ends:
No doubt he would have been much more pathetic,
But the sea acted as a strong emetic.

[After his ship is wrecked, Juan is washed up on a Greek island
and cared for by Haidee, a pirate's daughter]

177

It was a wild and breaker-beaten coast,
    With cliffs above, and a broad sandy shore,   1410
Guarded by shoals and rocks as by an host,
    With here and there a creek, whose aspect wore
A better welcome to the tempest-tost;
    And rarely ceased the haughty billow's roar,
Save on the dead long summer days, which make
The outstretch'd ocean glitter like a lake.

178

And the small ripple spilt upon the beach
    Scarcely o'erpass'd the cream of your champaigne,
When o'er the brim the sparkling bumpers reach,
    That spring-dew of the spirit! the heart's rain!   1420
Few things surpass old wine; and they may preach
    Who please, – the more because they preach in vain, –
Let us have wine and woman, mirth and laughter,
Sermons and soda water the day after.

179

Man, being reasonable, must get drunk;
    The best of life is but intoxication:

Glory, the grape, love, gold, in these are sunk
    The hopes of all men, and of every nation;
Without their sap, how branchless were the trunk
    Of life's strange tree, so fruitful on occasion: 1430
But to return, – Get very drunk; and when
You wake with head-ache, you shall see what then.

180

Ring for your valet – bid him quickly bring
    Some hock and soda-water, then you'll know
A pleasure worthy Xerxes the great king;
    For not the blest sherbet, sublimed with snow,
    Nor the first sparkle of the desert-spring,
    Nor Burgundy in all its sunset glow,
After long travel, ennui, love, or slaughter,
Vie with that draught of hock and soda-water.   1440

181

The coast – I think it was the coast that I
    Was just describing – Yes, it *was* the coast –
Lay at this period quiet as the sky,
    The sands untumbled, the blue waves untost,
And all was stillness, save the sea-bird's cry,
    And dolphin's leap, and little billow crost
By some low rock or shelve, that made it fret
Against the boundary it scarcely wet.

182

And forth they wandered, her sire being gone,
    As I have said, upon an expedition;   1450
And mother, brother, guardian, she had none,
    Save Zoe, who, although with due precision
She waited on her lady with the sun,
    Thought daily service was her only mission,
Bringing warm water, wreathing her long tresses,
And asking now and then for cast-off dresses.

183

It was the cooling hour, just when the rounded
    Red sun sinks down behind the azure hill,

Which then seems as if the whole earth it bounded,
　　Circling all nature, hush'd, and dim, and still,   1460
With the far mountain-crescent half surrounded
　　On one side, and the deep sea calm and chill
Upon the other, and the rosy sky,
With one star sparkling through it like an eye.

184

And thus they wander'd forth, and hand in hand,
　　Over the shining pebbles and the shells,
Glided along the smooth and harden'd sand,
　　And in the worn and wild receptacles
Work'd by the storms, yet work'd as it were plann'd,
　　In hollow halls, with sparry roofs and cells,   1470
They turn'd to rest; and, each clasp'd by an arm,
Yielded to the deep twilight's purple charm.

185

They look'd up to the sky, whose floating glow
　　Spread like a rosy ocean, vast and bright;
They gazed upon the glittering sea below,
　　Whence the broad moon rose circling into sight;
They heard the wave's splash, and the wind so low,
　　And saw each other's dark eyes darting light
Into each other – and, beholding this,
Their lips drew near, and clung into a kiss;   1480

186

A long, long kiss, a kiss of youth and love,
　　And beauty, all concentrating like rays
Into one focus, kindled from above;
　　Such kisses as belong to early days,
Where heart, and soul, and sense, in concert move,
　　And the blood's lava, and the pulse a blaze,
Each kiss a heart-quake, – for a kiss's strength,
I think, it must be reckon'd by its length.

187

By length I mean duration; theirs endured
　　Heaven knows how long – no doubt they never reckon'd;   1490

And if they had, they could not have secured
　　The sum of their sensations to a second:
They had not spoken; but they felt allured,
　　As if their souls and lips each other beckon'd,
Which, being join'd, like swarming bees they clung –
Their hearts the flowers from whence the honey sprung.

188

They were alone, but not alone as they
　　Who shut in chambers think it loneliness;
The silent ocean, and the starlight bay,
　　The twilight glow, which momently grew less,   1500
The voiceless sands, and dropping caves, that lay
　　Around them, made them to each other press,
As if there were no life beneath the sky
Save theirs, and that their life could never die.

189

They fear'd no eyes nor ears on that lone beach,
　　They felt no terrors from the night, they were
All in all to each other: though their speech
　　Was broken words, they *thought* a language there, –
And all the burning tongues the passions teach
　　Found in one sigh the best interpreter   1510
Of nature's oracle – first love, – that all
Which Eve has left her daughters since her fall.

190

Haidee spoke not of scruples, ask'd no vows,
　　Nor offer'd any; she had never heard
Of plight and promises to be a spouse,
　　Or perils by a loving maid incurr'd;
She was all which pure ignorance allows,
　　And flew to her young mate like a young bird;
And, never having dreamt of falsehood, she
Had not one word to say of constancy.   1520

191

She loved, and was beloved – she adored,
　　And she was worshipp'd; after nature's fashion,

Their intense souls, into each other pour'd,
    If souls could die, had perish'd in that passion, –
But by degrees their senses were restored,
    Again to be o'ercome, again to dash on;
And, beating 'gainst *his* bosom, Haidee's heart
Felt as if never more to beat apart.

192

Alas! they were so young, so beautiful,
    So lonely, loving, helpless, and the hour   1530
Was that in which the heart is always full,
    And, having o'er itself no further power,
Prompts deeds eternity can not annul,
    But pays off moments in an endless shower
Of hell-fire – all prepared for people giving
Pleasure or pain to one another living.

193

Alas! for Juan and Haidee! they were
    So loving and so lovely – till then never,
Excepting our first parents, such a pair
    Had run the risk of being damn'd for ever;   1540
And Haidee, being devout as well as fair,
    Had, doubtless, heard about the Stygian river,
And hell and purgatory – but forgot
Just in the very crisis she should not.

194

They look upon each other, and their eyes
    Gleam in the moonlight; and her white arm clasps
Round Juan's head, and his around hers lies
    Half buried in the tresses which it grasps;
She sits upon his knee, and drinks his sighs,
    He hers, until they end in broken gasps;   1550
And thus they form a group that's quite antique,
Half naked, loving, natural, and Greek.

195

And when those deep and burning moments pass'd,
    And Juan sunk to sleep within her arms,

She slept not, but all tenderly, though fast,
   Sustain'd his head upon her bosom's charms;
And now and then her eye to heaven is cast,
   And then on the pale cheek her breast now warms,
Pillow'd on her o'erflowing heart, which pants
With all it granted, and with all it grants.   1560

196

An infant when it gazes on a light,
   A child the moment when it drains the breast,
A devotee when soars the Host in sight,
   An Arab with a stranger for a guest,
A sailor when the prize has struck in fight,
   A miser filling his most hoarded chest,
Feel rapture; but not such true joy are reaping
As they who watch o'er what they love while sleeping.

197

For there it lies so tranquil, so beloved,
   All that it hath of life with us is living;   1570
So gentle, stirless, helpless, and unmoved,
   And all unconscious of the joy 'tis giving;
All it hath felt, inflicted, pass'd, and proved,
   Hush'd into depths beyond the watcher's diving;
There lies the thing we love with all its errors
And all its charms, like death without its terrors.

198

The lady watch'd her lover – and that hour
   Of Love's and Night's, and Ocean's solitude,
O'erflow'd her soul with their united power;
   Amidst the barren sand and rocks so rude   1580
She and her wave-worn love had made their bower,
   Where nought upon their passion could intrude,
And all the stars that crowded the blue space
Saw nothing happier than her glowing face.

199

Alas! the love of women! it is known
   To be a lovely and a fearful thing;

For all of theirs upon that die is thrown,
    And if 'tis lost, life hath no more to bring
To them but mockeries of the past alone,
    And their revenge is as the tiger's spring,   1590
Deadly, and quick, and crushing; yet, as real
Torture is theirs, what they inflict they feel.

200

They are right; for man, to man so oft unjust,
    Is always so to women; one sole bond
Awaits them, treachery is all their trust;
    Taught to conceal, their bursting hearts despond
Over their idol, till some wealthier lust
    Buys them in marriage – and what rests beyond?
A thankless husband, next a faithless lover,
Then dressing, nursing, praying, and all's over.   1600

201

Some take a lover, some take drams or prayers,
    Some mind their household, others dissipation,
Some run away, and but exchange their cares,
    Losing the advantage of a virtuous station;
Few changes e'er can better their affairs,
    Theirs being an unnatural situation,
From the dull palace to the dirty hovel:
Some play the devil, and then write a novel.

202

Haidee was Nature's bride, and knew not this;
    Haidee was Passion's child, born where the sun   1610
Showers triple light, and scorches even the kiss
    Of his gazelle-eyed daughters; she was one
Made but to love, to feel that she was his
    Who was her chosen: what was said or done
Elsewhere was nothing – She had nought to fear,
Hope, care, nor love beyond, her heart beat *here*.

203

And oh! that quickening of the heart, that beat!
    How much it costs us! yet each rising throb

Is in its cause as its effect so sweet,
    That Wisdom, ever on the watch to rob   1620
Joy of its alchymy, and to repeat
    Fine truths, even Conscience, too, has a tough job
To make us understand each good old maxim,
So good – I wonder Castlereagh don't tax 'em.

204

And now 'twas done – on the lone shore were plighted
    Their hearts; the stars, their nuptial torches, shed
Beauty upon the beautiful they lighted:
    Ocean their witness, and the cave their bed,
By their own feelings hallow'd and united,
    Their priest was Solitude, and they were wed: 1630
And they were happy, for to their young eyes
Each was an angel, and earth paradise.

205

Oh Love! of whom great Caesar was the suitor,
    Titus the master, Antony the slave,
Horace, Catullus, scholars, Ovid tutor,
    Sappho the sage blue-stocking, in whose grave
All those may leap who rather would be neuter –
    (Leucadia's rock still overlooks the wave)
Oh Love! thou art the very god of evil,
For, after all, we cannot call thee devil.   1640

206

Thou mak'st the chaste connubial state precarious,
    And jestest with the brows of mightiest men:
Caesar and Pompey, Mahomet, Belisarius,
    Have much employ'd the muse of history's pen;
Their lives and fortunes were extremely various,
    Such worthies Time will never see again;
Yet to these four in three things the same luck holds,
They all were heroes, conquerors, and cuckolds.

207

Thou mak'st philosophers; there's Epicurus
    And Aristippus, a material crew!   1650

Who to immoral courses would allure us
   By theories quite practicable too;
If only from the devil they would insure us,
   How pleasant were the maxim, (not quite new)
'Eat, drink, and love, what can the rest avail us?'
So said the royal sage Sardanapalus.

208

But Juan! had he quite forgotten Julia?
   And should he have forgotten her so soon?
I can't but say it seems to me most truly a
   Perplexing question; but, no doubt, the moon   1660
Does these things for us, and whenever newly a
   Strong palpitation rises, 'tis her boon,
Else how the devil is it that fresh features
Have such a charm for us poor human creatures?

209

I hate inconstancy – I loathe, detest,
   Abhor, condemn, abjure the mortal made
Of such quicksilver clay that in his breast
   No permanent foundation can be laid;
Love, constant love, has been my constant guest,
   And yet last night, being at a masquerade,   1670
I saw the prettiest creature, fresh from Milan,
Which gave me some sensations like a villain.

210

But soon Philosophy came to my aid,
   And whisper'd 'think of every sacred tie!'
'I will, my dear Philosophy!' I said,
   'But then her teeth, and then, Oh heaven! her eye!
I'll just inquire if she be wife or maid,
   Or neither – out of curiosity.'
'Stop!' cried Philosophy, with air so Grecian,
(Though she was masqued then as a fair Venetian.)   1680

211

'Stop!' so I stopp'd. – But to return: that which
   Men call inconstancy is nothing more

Than admiration due where nature's rich
 Profusion with young beauty covers o'er
Some favour'd object; and as in the niche
 A lovely statue we almost adore,
This sort of adoration of the real
Is but a heightening of the 'beau ideal.'

212

'Tis the perception of the beautiful,
 A fine extension of the faculties,   1690
Platonic, universal, wonderful,
 Drawn from the stars, and filter'd through the skies,
Without which life would be extremely dull;
 In short, it is the use of our own eyes,
With one or two small senses added, just
To hint that flesh is form'd of fiery dust.

213

Yet 'tis a painful feeling, and unwilling,
 For surely if we always could perceive
In the same object graces quite as killing
 As when she rose upon us like an Eve,   1700
'Twould save us many a heart-ache, many a shilling,
 (For we must get them any how, or grieve,)
Whereas if one sole lady pleased for ever,
How pleasant for the heart, as well as liver!

214

The heart is like the sky, a part of heaven,
 But changes night and day too, like the sky;
Now o'er it clouds and thunder must be driven,
 And darkness and destruction as on high:
But when it hath been scorch'd, and pierced, and riven,
 Its storms expire in water-drops; the eye 1710
Pours forth at last the heart's-blood turn'd to tears,
Which make the English climate of our years.

215

The liver is the lazaret of bile,
 But very rarely executes its function,

For the first passion stays there such a while,
    That all the rest creep in and form a junction,
Like knots of vipers on a dunghill's soil,
    Rage, fear, hate, jealousy, revenge, compunction,
So that all mischiefs spring up from this entrail,
Like earthquakes from the hidden fire call'd 'central.'   1720

216

In the mean time, without proceeding more
    In this anatomy, I've finish'd now
Two hundred and odd stanzas as before,
    That being about the number I'll allow
Each canto of the twelve, or twenty-four;
    And, laying down my pen, I make my bow,
Leaving Don Juan and Haidee to plead
For them and theirs with all who deign to read.

from Don Juan Canto VIII

[Sold into slavery by Haidee's father, Juan escapes and finds
himself caught up in Russian attempts to storm a Turkish
fortress]

1

Oh blood and thunder! and oh blood and wounds! –
    These are but vulgar oaths, as you may deem,
Too gentle reader! and most shocking sounds:
    And so they are; yet thus is Glory's dream
Unriddled, and as my true Muse expounds
    At present such things, since they are her theme,
So be they her inspirers! Call them Mars,
Bellona, what you will – they mean but wars.

2

All was prepared – the fire, the sword, the men
    To wield them in their terrible array.   10

The army, like a lion from his den,
  Marched forth with nerve and sinews bent to slay, –
A human Hydra, issuing from its fen
  To breathe destruction on its winding way,
Whose heads were heroes, which cut off in vain
Immediately in others grew again.

3

History can only take things in the gross;
  But could we know them in detail, perchance
In balancing the profit and the loss,
  War's merit it by no means might enhance,   20
To waste so much gold for a little dross,
  As hath been done, mere conquest to advance.
The drying up a single tear has more
Of honest fame, than shedding seas of gore.

4

And why? – because it brings self-approbation;
  Whereas the other, after all its glare,
Shouts, bridges, arches, pensions from a nation, –
  Which (it may be) has not much left to spare, –
A higher title, or a loftier station,
  Though they may make Corruption gape or stare,   30
Yet, in the end, except in freedom's battles,
Are nothing but a child of Murder's rattles.

5

And such they are – and such they will be found.
  Not so Leonidas and Washington,
Whose every battle-field is holy ground,
  Which breathes of nations saved, not worlds undone.
How sweetly on the ear such echoes sound!
  While the mere victor's may appal or stun
The servile and the vain, such names will be
A watchword till the future shall be free.   40

6

The night was dark, and the thick mist allowed
  Nought to be seen save the artillery's flame,

Which arched the horizon like a fiery cloud,
   And in the Danube's waters shone the same –
A mirrored Hell! The volleying roar, and loud
   Long booming of each peal on peal, o'ercame
The ear far more than thunder; for Heaven's flashes
Spare, or smite rarely – Man's make millions ashes! [...]

82

The city's taken – only part by part –
   And Death is drunk with gore: there's not a street   650
Where fights not to the last some desperate heart
   For those for whom it soon shall cease to beat.
Here War forgot his own destructive Art
   In more destroying Nature; and, the heat
Of Carnage, like the Nile's sun-sodden Slime,
Engendered monstrous shapes of every Crime.

83

A Russian officer, in martial tread
   Over a heap of bodies, felt his heel
Seized fast, as if 'twere by the serpent's head
   Whose fangs Eve taught her human seed to feel: 660
In vain he kicked, and swore, and writhed, and bled,
   And howled for help as wolves do for a meal –
The teeth still kept their gratifying hold,
As do the subtle snakes described of old.

84

A dying Moslem, who had felt the foot
   Of a foe o'er him, snatched at it, and bit
The very tendon, which is most acute –
   (That which some ancient Muse or modern Wit
Named after thee, Achilles) and quite through 't
   He made the teeth meet, nor relinquish'd it   670
Even with his life – for (but they lie) 'tis said
To the live leg still clung the severed head.

85

However this may be, 'tis pretty sure
   The Russian officer for life was lamed,

For the Turk's teeth stuck faster than a skewer,
   And left him 'midst the invalid and maimed:
The regimental surgeon could not cure
   His patient, and perhaps was to be blamed
More than the head of the inveterate foe,
Which was cut off, and scarce even then let go.   680

86

But then the fact's a fact – and 'tis the part
   Of a true poet to escape from fiction
Whene'er he can; for there is little art
   In leaving verse more free from the restriction
Of truth than prose, unless to suit the mart
   For what is sometimes called poetic diction,
And that outrageous appetite for lies
Which Satan angles with, for souls, like flies.

87

The city's taken, but not rendered! – No!
   There's not a Moslem that hath yielded sword: 690
The blood may gush out, as the Danube's flow
   Rolls by the city wall; but deed nor word
Acknowledge aught of dread of death or foe:
   In vain the yell of victory is roared
By the advancing Muscovite – the groan
Of the last foe is echoed by his own.

88

The bayonet pierces and the sabre cleaves,
   And human lives are lavished every where,
As the year closing whirls the scarlet leaves
   When the stript forest bows to the bleak air,   700
And groans; and thus the peopled City grieves,
   Shorn of its best and loveliest, and left bare;
But still it falls with vast and awful splinters,
As Oaks blown down with all their thousand winters.

89

It is an awful topic – but 'tis not
   My cue for any time to be terrific:

For checquered as is seen our human lot
   With good, and bad, and worse, alike prolific
Of melancholy merriment, to quote
   Too much of one sort would be soporific; –   710
Without, or with, offence to friends or foes,
I sketch your world exactly as it goes.

90

And one good action in the midst of crimes
   Is 'quite refreshing,' in the affected phrase
Of these ambrosial, Pharisaic times,
   With all their pretty milk-and-water ways,
And may serve therefore to bedew these rhymes,
   A little scorched at present with the blaze
Of conquest and its consequences, which
Make Epic poesy so rare and rich.   720

91

Upon a taken bastion where there lay
   Thousands of slaughtered men, a yet warm group
Of murdered women, who had found their way
   To this vain refuge, made the good heart droop
And shudder; – while, as beautiful as May,
   A female child of ten years tried to stoop
And hide her little palpitating breast
Amidst the bodies lulled in bloody rest.

92

Two villainous Cossacques pursued the child
   With flashing eyes and weapons: matched with them   730
The rudest brute that roams Siberia's wild
   Has feelings pure and polished as a gem, –
The bear is civilized, the wolf is mild:
   And whom for this at last must we condemn?
Their natures? or their sovereigns, who employ
All arts to teach their subjects to destroy?

93

Their sabres glittered o'er her little head,
   Whence her fair hair rose twining with affright,

Her hidden face was plunged amidst the dead:
   When Juan caught a glimpse of this sad sight,   740
I shall not say exactly what he *said*,
   Because it might not solace 'ears polite;'
But what he *did*, was to lay on their backs,
The readiest way of reasoning with Cossacques.

94

One's hip he slashed, and split the other's shoulder,
   And drove them with their brutal yells to seek
If there might be chirurgeons who could solder
   The wounds they richly merited, and shriek
Their baffled rage and pain; while waxing colder
   As he turned o'er each pale and gory cheek,   750
Don Juan raised his little captive from
The heap a moment more had made her tomb.

95

And she was chill as they, and on her face
   A slender streak of blood announced how near
Her fate had been to that of all her race;
   For the same blow which laid her Mother here,
Had scarred her brow, and left its crimson trace
   As the last link with all she had held dear;
But else unhurt, she opened her large eyes,
And gazed on Juan with a wild surprise.   760

96

Just at this instant, while their eyes were fixed
   Upon each other, with dilated glance,
In Juan's look, pain, pleasure, hope, fear, mixed
   With joy to save, and dread of some mischance
Unto his protégée; while hers, transfixed
   With infant terrors, glared as from a trance,
A pure, transparent, pale, yet radiant face,
Like to a lighted alabaster vase; –

97

Up came John Johnson: (I will not say '*Jack*,'
   For that were vulgar, cold, and common place   770

On great occasions, such as an attack
    On cities, as hath been the present case:)
Up Johnson came, with hundreds at his back,
    Exclaiming: – 'Juan! Juan! On, boy! brace
Your arm, and I'll bet Moscow to a dollar
That you and I will win St. George's collar.

98

'The Seraskier is knocked upon the head,
    But the stone bastion still remains, wherein
The old Pacha sits among some hundreds dead,
    Smoking his pipe quite calmly 'midst the din   780
Of our artillery and his own: 'tis said
    Our killed, already piled up to the chin,
Lie round the battery; but still it batters,
And grape in volleys, like a vineyard, scatters.

99

'Then up with me!' – But Juan answered, 'Look
    Upon this child – I saved her – must not leave
Her life to chance; but point me out some nook
    Of safety, where she less may shrink and grieve,
And I am with you.' – Whereon Johnson took
    A glance around – and shrugged – and twitched his sleeve   790
And black silk neckcloth – and replied, 'You're right;
Poor thing! what's to be done? I'm puzzled quite.'

100

Said Juan – 'Whatsoever is to be
    Done, I'll not quit her till she seems secure
Of present life a good deal more than we.' –
    Quoth Johnson – '*Neither* will I quite ensure;
But at the least *you* may die gloriously.' –
    Juan replied – 'At least I will endure
Whate'er is to be borne – but not resign
This child, who is parentless and therefore mine.'   800

101

Johnson said – 'Juan, we've no time to lose;
    The child's a pretty child – a very pretty –

I never saw such eyes – but hark! now choose
  Between your fame and feelings, pride and pity; –
Hark! how the roar increases! – no excuse
  Will serve when there is plunder in a city: –
I should be loth to march without you, but,
By God! we'll be too late for the first cut.'

102

But Juan was immoveable; until
  Johnson, who really loved him in his way,   810
Picked out amongst his followers with some skill
  Such as he thought the least given up to prey;
And swearing if the infant came to ill
  That they should all be shot on the next day;
But, if she were delivered safe and sound,
They should at least have fifty roubles round;

from **Don Juan Canto IX**

[Byron addresses the Duke of Wellington
and other English readers]

1

Oh, Wellington! (or 'Vilainton' – for Fame
  Sounds the heroic syllables both ways;
France could not even conquer your great name,
  But punned it down to this facetious phrase –
Beating or beaten she will laugh the same) –
  You have obtained great pensions and much praise;
Glory like yours should any dare gainsay,
Humanity would rise, and thunder 'Nay!'

2

I don't think that you used K[in]n[ai]rd quite well
  In Marinêt's affair – in fact 'twas shabby,   10
And like some other things won't do to tell

Upon your tomb in Westminster's old abbey.
Upon the rest 'tis not worth while to dwell,
　　Such tales being for the tea hours of some tabby;
But though your years as *man* tend fast to zero,
In fact your Grace is still but a *young Hero.*

3

Though Britain owes (and pays you too) so much,
　　Yet Europe doubtless owes you greatly more:
You have repaired Legitimacy's crutch, –
　　A prop not quite so certain as before: 20
The Spanish, and the French, as well as Dutch,
　　Have seen, and felt, how strongly you *restore*;
And Waterloo has made the world your debtor –
(I wish your bards would sing it rather better.)

4

You are 'the best of cut-throats:' – do not start;
　　The phrase is Shakespeare's, and not misapplied: –
War's a brain-spattering, windpipe-slitting art,
　　Unless her cause by Right be sanctified.
If you have acted *once* a generous part,
　　The World, not the World's masters, will decide,   30
And I shall be delighted to learn who,
Save you and yours, have gained by Waterloo?

5

I am no flatterer – you've supped full of flattery:
　　They say you like it too – 'tis no great wonder:
He whose whole life has been assault and battery,
　　At last may get a little tired of thunder;
And swallowing eulogy much more than satire, he
　　May like being praised for every lucky blunder;
Called 'Saviour of the Nations' – not yet saved;
And Europe's Liberator – still enslaved.   40

6

I've done. Now go and dine from off the plate
　　Presented by the Prince of the Brazils,
And send the sentinel before your gate

A slice or two from your luxurious meals:
He fought, but has not fed so well of late.
 Some hunger too they say the people feels: –
There is no doubt that you deserved your ration,
But pray give back a little to the nation.

                            7

I don't mean to reflect – a man so great as
 You, my Lord Duke! is far above reflection.   50
The high Roman fashion too of Cincinnatus,
 With modern history has but small connection:
Though as an Irishman you love potatoes,
 You need not take them under your direction;
And half a million for your Sabine farm
Is rather dear! – I'm sure I mean no harm.

                            8

Great men have always scorned great recompenses:
 Epaminondas saved his Thebes, and died,
Not leaving even his funeral expenses:
 George Washington had thanks and nought beside,   60
Except the all-cloudless Glory (which few men's is)
 To free his country: Pitt too had his pride,
And, as a high-soul'd Minister of State, is
Renowned for ruining Great Britain gratis.

                            9

Never had mortal Man such opportunity,
 Except Napoleon, or abused it more:
You might have freed fall'n Europe from the Unity
 Of Tyrants, and been blest from shore to shore:
And *now* – What *is* your fame? Shall the Muse tune it ye?
 Now – that the rabble's first vain shouts are o'er?   70
Go, hear it in your famished Country's cries!
Behold the World! and curse your victories!

                            10

As these new Cantos touch on warlike feats,
 To *you* the unflattering Muse deigns to inscribe
Truths that you will not read in the Gazettes,

But which, 'tis time to teach the hireling tribe
Who fatten on their Country's gore and debts,
    Must be recited, and – without a bribe.
You *did great* things; but not being *great* in mind,
Have left *undone* the *greatest* – and mankind.   80

                            11

Death laughs – Go ponder o'er the skeleton
    With which men image out the unknown thing
That hides the past world, like to a set sun
    Which still elsewhere may rouse a brighter spring, –
Death laughs at all you weep for: – look upon
    This hourly dread of all, whose *threatened sting*
Turns life to terror, even though in its sheath!
Mark! how its lipless mouth grins without breath!

                            12

Mark! how it laughs and scorns at all you are!
    And yet *was* what you are: from *ear* to *ear*   90
It *laughs not* – there is now no fleshy bar
    So called; the Antic long hath ceased to *hear*,
But still he *smiles*; and whether near or far
    He strips from man that mantle (far more dear
Than even the tailor's) his incarnate skin,
White, black, or copper – the dead bones will grin.

                            13

And thus Death laughs, – it is sad merriment,
    But still it *is* so; and with such example
Why should not Life be equally content,
    With his Superior, in a smile to trample   100
Upon the nothings which are daily spent
    Like bubbles on an ocean much less ample
Than the eternal deluge, which devours
Suns as rays – worlds like atoms – years like hours?

                            14

'To be or not to be! that is the question,'
    Says Shakespeare, who just now is much in fashion.
I am neither Alexander nor Hephaestion,

Nor ever had for *abstract* fame much passion;
But would much rather have a sound digestion,
   Than Buonaparte's cancer: – could I dash on   110
Through fifty victories to shame or fame,
Without a stomach – what were a good name?

15

'Oh dura ilia messorum!' – 'Oh
   Ye rigid guts of reapers!' – I translate
For the great benefit of those who know
   What Indigestion is – that inward fate
Which makes all Styx through one small liver flow.
   A peasant's sweat is worth his Lord's estate:
Let *this* one toil for bread – *that* rack for rent,
He who sleeps best, may be the most content.   120

16

'To be or not to be?'– Ere I decide,
   I should be glad to know that which *is being?*
'Tis true we speculate both far and wide,
   And deem, because we *see*, we are *all-seeing:*
For my part, I'll enlist on neither side,
   Until I see both sides for once agreeing.
For me, I sometimes think that Life is Death,
Rather than Life a mere affair of breath.

17

'Que sçais-je?' was the motto of Montaigne,
   As also of the first Academicians: 130
That all is dubious which Man may attain,
   Was one of their most favourite positions.
There's no such thing as certainty, that's plain
   As any of Mortality's Conditions:
So little do we know what we're about in
This world, I doubt if doubt itself be doubting.

18

It is a pleasant voyage perhaps to float,
   Like Pyrrho, on a sea of speculation;
But what if carrying sail capsize the boat?

Your wise men don't know much of navigation;   140
And swimming long in the abyss of thought
    Is apt to tire: a calm and shallow station
Well nigh the shore, where one stoops down and gathers
Some pretty shell, is best for moderate bathers.

19

'But Heaven,' as Cassio says, 'is above all, –
    No more of this then, – let us pray!' We have
Souls to save, since Eve's slip and Adam's fall,
    Which tumbled all mankind into the grave,
Besides fish, beasts, and birds. 'The Sparrow's fall
    Is special providence,' though how *it* gave   150
Offence, we know not; probably it perched
Upon the tree which Eve so fondly searched.

20

Oh, ye immortal Gods! what is Theogony?
    Oh, thou too mortal Man! what is Philanthropy?
Oh, World! which was and is, what is Cosmogony?
    Some people have accused me of Misanthropy;
And yet I know no more than the mahogany
    That forms this desk, of what they mean: – *Lykanthropy*
I comprehend, for without transformation
Men become wolves on any slight occasion.   160

21

But I, the mildest, meekest of mankind,
    Like Moses, or Melancthon, who have ne'er
Done any thing exceedingly unkind, –
    And (though I could not now and then forbear
Following the bent of body or of mind)
    Have always had a tendency to spare, –
Why do they call me misanthrope? Because
They hate me, not I them: – And here we'll pause.

from **Don Juan Canto XI**

[Juan is now in England and Byron reflects on
his own 'Years of Fame']

55

In twice five years the 'greatest living poet,'
  Like to the champion in the fisty ring,
Is called on to support his claim, or show it,
  Although 'tis an imaginary thing.
Even I – albeit I'm sure I did not know it,
  Nor sought of foolscap subjects to be king, –
Was reckoned, a considerable time,
The grand Napoleon of the realms of rhyme.   440

56

But Juan was my Moscow, and Faliero
  My Leipsic, and my Mont Saint Jean seems Cain:
'La Belle Alliance' of dunces down at zero,
  Now that the Lion's fall'n, may rise again:
But I will fall at least as fell my hero;
  Nor reign at all, or as a *monarch* reign;
Or to some lonely isle of Jailors go,
With turncoat Southey for my turnkey Lowe.

57

Sir Walter reigned before me; Moore and Campbell
  Before and after; but now grown more holy,   450
The Muses upon Sion's hill must ramble,
  With poets almost clergymen, or wholly;
And Pegasus hath a psalmodic amble
  Beneath the reverend Cambyses Croly,
Who shoes the glorious animal with stilts,
A modern Ancient Pistol – 'by these Hilts!'

58

Still he excels that artificial hard
  Labourer in the same vineyard, though the vine
Yields him but vinegar for his reward, –
  That neutralised dull Dorus of the Nine;   460

That swarthy Sporus, neither man nor bard;
   That ox of verse, who *ploughs* for every line: –
Cambyses' roaring Romans beat at least
The howling Hebrews of Cybele's priest. –

59

Then there's my gentle Euphues; who, they say,
   Sets up for being a sort of *moral me*;
He'll find it rather difficult some day
   To turn out both, or either, it may be.
Some persons think that Coleridge hath the sway;
   And Wordsworth has supporters, two or three;   470
And that deep-mouthed Boeotian, 'Savage Landor,'
Has taken for a swan rogue Southey's gander.

60

John Keats, who was killed off by one critique,
   Just as he really promised something great,
If not intelligible, – without Greek
   Contrived to talk about the Gods of late,
Much as they might have been supposed to speak.
   Poor fellow! His was an untoward fate: –
'Tis strange the mind, that very fiery particle,
Should let itself be snuffed out by an Article.   480

61

The list grows long of live and dead pretenders
   To that which none will gain – or none will know
The Conqueror at least; who, ere time renders
   His last award, will have the long grass grow
Above his burnt-out brain, and sapless cinders.
   If I might augur, I should rate but low
Their chances; – they're too numerous, like the thirty
Mock tyrants, when Rome's annals waxed but dirty.

62

This is the literary *lower* Empire,
   Where the Praetorian bands take up the matter; –   490
A 'dreadful trade,' like his who 'gathers samphire,'
   The insolent soldiery to soothe and flatter,

With the same feelings as you'd coax a vampire.
   Now, were I once at home, and in good satire,
I'd try conclusions with those Janizaries,
And show them *what* an intellectual war is.

63

I think I know a trick or two, would turn
   Their flanks; – but it is hardly worth my while
With such small gear to give myself concern:
   Indeed I've not the necessary bile;   500
My natural temper's really aught but stern,
   And even my Muse's worst reproof's a smile;
And then she drops a brief and modern curtsey,
And glides away, assured she never hurts ye.

64

My Juan, whom I left in deadly peril
   Amongst live poets and blue ladies, past
With some small profit through that field so sterile.
   Being tired in time, and neither least nor last
Left it before he had been treated very ill;
   And henceforth found himself more gaily classed   510
Amongst the higher spirits of the day,
The sun's true son, no vapour, but a ray.

65

His morns he passed in business – which dissected,
   Was like all business, a laborious nothing,
That leads to lassitude, the most infected
   And Centaur-Nessus garb of mortal clothing,
And on our sophas makes us lie dejected,
   And talk in tender horrors of our loathing
All kinds of toil, save for our country's good –
Which grows no better, though 'tis time it should.   520

66

His afternoons he passed in visits, luncheons,
   Lounging, and boxing; and the twilight hour
In riding round those vegetable puncheons
   Called 'Parks,' where there is neither fruit nor flower

Enough to gratify a bee's slight munchings;
   But after all it is the only 'bower,'
(In Moore's phrase) where the fashionable fair
Can form a slight acquaintance with fresh air.

67

Then dress, then dinner, then awakes the world!
   Then glare the lamps, then whirl the wheels, then roar   530
Through street and square fast flashing chariots, hurled
   Like harnessed meteors; then along the floor
Chalk mimics painting; then festoons are twirled;
   Then roll the brazen thunders of the door,
Which opens to the thousand happy few
An earthly Paradise of 'Or Molu.'

68

There stands the noble Hostess, nor shall sink
   With the three-thousandth curtsey; there the Waltz,
The only dance which teaches girls to think,
   Makes one in love even with its very faults.   540
Saloon, room, hall o'erflow beyond their brink,
   And long the latest of arrivals halts,
'Midst royal dukes and dames condemned to climb,
And gain an inch of staircase at a time.

69

Thrice happy he, who, after a survey
   Of the good company, can win a corner,
A door that's *in*, or boudoir *out* of the way,
   Where he may fix himself, like small 'Jack Horner,'
And let the Babel round run as it may,
   And look on as a mourner, or a scorner,   550
Or an approver, or a mere spectator,
Yawning a little as the night grows later.

70

But this won't do, save by and by; and he
   Who, like Don Juan, takes an active share,
Must steer with care through all that glittering sea
   Of gems and plumes, and pearls and silks, to where

He deems it is his proper place to be;
   Dissolving in the waltz to some soft air,
Or proudlier prancing with mercurial skill
Where Science marshals forth her own quadrille.   560

71

Or, if he dance not, but hath higher views
   Upon an heiress or his neighbour's bride,
Let him take care that that which he pursues
   Is not at once too palpably descried.
Full many an eager gentleman oft rues
   His haste: impatience is a blundering guide
Amongst a people famous for reflection,
Who like to play the fool with circumspection.

72

But, if you can contrive, get next at supper;
   Or, if forestalled, get opposite and ogle: –   570
Oh, ye ambrosial moments! always upper
   In mind, a sort of sentimental bogle,
Which sits for ever upon Memory's crupper,
   The ghost of vanished pleasures once in vogue! Ill
Can tender souls relate the rise and fall
Of hopes and fears which shake a single ball.

73

But these precautionary hints can touch
   Only the common run, who must pursue,
And watch, and ward; whose plans a word too much
   Or little overturns; and not the few   580
Or many (for the number's sometimes such)
   Whom a good mien, especially if new,
Or fame, or name, for wit, war, sense, or nonsense,
Permits whate'er they please, or *did* not long since.

74

Our hero, as a hero, young and handsome,
   Noble, rich, celebrated, and a stranger,
Like other slaves of course must pay his ransom
   Before he can escape from so much danger

As will environ a conspicuous man. Some
    Talk about poetry, and 'rack and manger,'   590
And ugliness, disease, as toil and trouble, –
I wish they knew the life of a young noble.

75

They are young, but know not youth – it is anticipated;
    Handsome but wasted, rich without a sou;
Their vigour in a thousand arms is dissipated;
    Their cash comes *from*, their wealth goes *to* a Jew;
Both senates see their nightly votes participated
    Between the tyrant's and the tribunes' crew;
And having voted, dined, drank, gamed, and whored,
The family vault receives another lord.   600

76

'Where is the world,' cries Young, at *eighty?* 'Where
    The world in which a man was born?' Alas!
Where is the world of *eight* years past? *'Twas there* –
    I look for it – 'tis gone, a Globe of Glass!
Cracked, shivered, vanished, scarcely gazed on, ere
    A silent change dissolves the glittering mass.
Statesmen, chiefs, orators, queens, patriots, kings,
And dandies, all are gone on the wind's wings.

77

Where is Napoleon the Grand? God knows:
    Where little Castlereagh? The devil can tell: 610
Where Grattan, Curran, Sheridan, all those
    Who bound the bar or senate in their spell?
Where is the unhappy Queen, with all her woes?
    And where the Daughter, whom the Isles loved well?
Where are those martyred Saints the Five per Cents?
And where – oh where the devil are the Rents!

78

Where's Brummell? Dished. Where's Long Pole Wellesley? Diddled.
    Where's Whitbread? Romilly? Where's George the Third?
Where is his will? (That's not so soon unriddled.)
    And where is 'Fum' the Fourth, our 'royal bird?'   620

Gone down it seems to Scotland, to be fiddled
    Unto by Sawney's violin, we have heard:
'Caw me, caw thee' – for six months hath been hatching
This scene of royal itch and loyal scratching.

79

Where is Lord This? And where my Lady That?
    The Honourable Mistresses and Misses?
Some laid aside like an old opera hat,
    Married, unmarried, and remarried: (this is
An evolution oft performed of late).
    Where are the Dublin shouts – and London hisses?   630
Where are the Grenvilles? Turned as usual. Where
My friends the Whigs? Exactly where they were.

80

Where are the Lady Carolines and Franceses?
    Divorced or doing thereanent. Ye annals
So brilliant, where the list of routs and dances is, –
    Thou Morning Post, sole record of the pannels
Broken in carriages, and all the phantasies
    Of fashion, – say what streams now fill those channels?
Some die, some fly, some languish on the Continent,
Because the times have hardly left them *one* tenant.   640

81

Some who once set their caps at cautious Dukes,
    Have taken up at length with younger brothers:
Some heiresses have bit at sharpers' hooks;
    Some maids have been made wives, some merely mothers;
Others have lost their fresh and fairy looks:
    In short, the list of alterations bothers:
There's little strange in this, but something strange is
The unusual quickness of these common changes.

82

Talk not of seventy years as age! in seven
    I have seen more changes, down from monarchs to   650
The humblest individual under heaven,
    Than might suffice a moderate century through.

I knew that nought was lasting, but now even
   Change grows too changeable, without being new:
Nought's permanent among the human race,
Except the Whigs *not* getting into place.

83

I have seen Napoleon, who seemed quite a Jupiter,
   Shrink to a Saturn. I have seen a Duke
(No matter which) turn politician stupider,
   If that can well be, than his wooden look.   660
But it is time that I should hoist my 'blue Peter,'
   And sail for a new theme: – I have seen – and shook
To see it – the King hissed, and then carest;
But don't pretend to settle which was best.

84

I have seen the landholders without a rap
   I have seen Johanna Southcote – I have seen
The House of Commons turned to a tax-trap –
   I have seen that sad affair of the late Queen
I have seen crowns worn instead of a fool's-cap –
   I have seen a Congress doing all that's mean –   670
I have seen some nations like o'erloaded asses
Kick off their burthens – meaning the high classes.

85

I have seen small poets, and great prosers, and
   Interminable – *not eternal* – speakers –
I have seen the Funds at war with house and land –
   I've seen the Country Gentlemen turn squeakers –
I've seen the people ridden o'er like sand
   By slaves on horseback – I have seen malt liquors
Exchanged for 'thin potations' by John Bull –
I have seen John half detect himself a fool. –   680

86

But 'Carpe diem,' Juan, 'Carpe, carpe!'
   To-morrow sees another race as gay
And transient, and devoured by the same harpy.

'Life's a poor player,' – then 'play out the play,
Ye villains!' and above all keep a sharp eye
    Much less on what you do than what you say:
Be hypocritical, be cautious, be
Not what you *seem*, but always what you *see*.

87

But how shall I relate in other Cantos
    Of what befell our hero in the land,   690
Which 'tis the common cry and lie to vaunt as
    A moral country? But I hold my hand –
For I disdain to write an Atalantis;
    But 'tis as well at once to understand,
You are *not* a moral people, and you know it
Without the aid of too sincere a poet.

from Don Juan Canto XVI

[In the English country house where he is a guest
Juan thinks he has seen a ghost]

110

And full of sentiments, sublime as billows
    Heaving between this world and worlds beyond,
Don Juan, when the midnight hour of pillows
    Arrived, retired to his; but to despond
Rather than rest. Instead of poppies, willows
    Waved o'er his couch; he meditated, fond
Of those sweet bitter thoughts which banish sleep,
And make the worldling sneer, the youngling weep.

111

The night was as before: he was undrest,
    Saving his night gown, which is an undress;   930
Completely 'sans culotte,' and without vest;
    In short, he hardly could be clothed with less;
But apprehensive of his spectral guest,

He sate, with feelings awkward to express,
(By those who have not had such visitations)
Expectant of the ghost's fresh operations.

112

And not in vain he listened – Hush! what's that?
　　I see – I see – Ah, no! – 'tis not – yet 'tis –
Ye powers! it is the – the – the – Pooh! the cat!
　　The devil may take that stealthy pace of his!　　　940
So like a spiritual pit-a-pat,
　　Or tiptoe of an amatory Miss,
Gliding the first time to a rendezvous,
And dreading the chaste echoes of her shoe.

113

Again – what is't? The wind? No, no, – this time
　　It is the sable Friar as before,
With awful footsteps regular as rhyme,
　　Or (as rhymes may be in these days) much more.
Again, through shadows of the night sublime,
　　When deep sleep fell on men, and the world wore　　950
The starry darkness round her like a girdle
Spangled with gems – the monk made his blood curdle.

114

A noise like to wet fingers drawn on glass,
　　Which sets the teeth on edge; and a slight clatter
Like showers which on the midnight gusts will pass,
　　Sounding like very supernatural water,
Came over Juan's ear, which throbbed, alas!
　　For immaterialism's a serious matter;
So that even those whose faith is the most great
In souls immortal, shun them tête-à-tête.　　　960

115

Were his eyes open? – Yes! and his mouth too.
　　Surprise has this effect – to make one dumb,
Yet leave the gate which Eloquence slips through
　　As wide as if a long speech were to come.
Nigh and more nigh the awful echoes drew,

Tremendous to a mortal tympanum:
His eyes were open, and (as was before
Stated) his mouth. What opened next? – the door.

116

It opened with a most infernal creak,
    Like that of Hell. 'Lasciate ogni speranza   970
Voi che entrate!' The hinge seemed to speak,
    Dreadful as Dante's Rima, or this stanza;
Or – but all words upon such themes are weak;
    A single shade's sufficient to entrance a
Hero – for what is substance to a Spirit?
Or how is't *matter* trembles to come near it?

117

The door flew wide, not swiftly – but, as fly
    The sea-gulls, with a steady, sober flight –
And then swung back; nor close – but stood awry,
    Half letting in long shadows on the light,   980
Which still in Juan's candlesticks burned high,
    For he had two, both tolerably bright,
And in the door-way, darkening Darkness, stood
The sable Friar in his solemn hood.

118

Don Juan shook, as erst he had been shaken
    The night before; but being sick of shaking,
He first inclined to think he had been mistaken,
    And then to be ashamed of such mistaking;
His own internal ghost began to awaken
    Within him, and to quell his corporal quaking –   990
Hinting that soul and body on the whole
Were odds against a disembodied soul.

119

And then his dread grew wrath, and his wrath fierce;
    And he arose, advanced – the shade retreated;
But Juan, eager now the truth to pierce,
    Followed, his veins no longer cold, but heated,
Resolved to thrust the mystery carte and tierce,

At whatsoever risk of being defeated:
The ghost stopped, menaced, then retired, until
He reached the ancient wall, then stood stone still.   1000

120

Juan put forth one arm – Eternal Powers!
   It touched no soul, nor body, but the wall,
On which the moonbeams fell in silvery showers
   Checquered with all the tracery of the hall;
He shuddered, as no doubt the bravest cowers
   When he can't tell what 'tis that doth appal.
How odd, a single hobgoblin's non-entity
Should cause more fear than a whole host's identity!

121

But still the shade remained; the blue eyes glared,
   And rather variably for stony death;   1010
Yet one thing rather good the grave had spared,
   The ghost had a remarkably sweet breath.
A straggling curl showed he had been fair-haired;
   A red lip, with two rows of pearls beneath,
Gleamed forth, as through the casement's ivy shroud
The moon peeped, just escaped from a grey cloud.

122

And Juan, puzzled, but still curious, thrust
   His other arm forth – Wonder upon wonder!
It pressed upon a hard but glowing bust,
   Which beat as if there was a warm heart under.   1020
He found, as people on most trials must,
   That he had made at first a silly blunder,
And that in his confusion he had caught
Only the wall, instead of what he sought.

123

The ghost, if ghost it were, seemed a sweet soul
   As ever lurked beneath a holy hood:
A dimpled chin, a neck of ivory, stole
   Forth into something much like flesh and blood;
Back fell the sable frock and dreary cowl,

And they revealed – alas! that e'er they should!   1030
In full, voluptuous, but *not o'er*grown bulk,
The phantom of her frolic Grace – Fitz-Fulke!

from Don Juan Canto XVII

[Byron picks up the story again]

6

Therefore I would solicit free discussion
   Upon all points no matter what, or whose –
Because as Ages upon Ages push on,
   The last is apt the former to accuse
Of pillowing its head on a pin-cushion,
   Heedless of pricks because it was obtuse:
What *was* a paradox becomes a truth or
A something like it – as bear witness Luther!

7

The Sacraments have been reduced to two,
   And Witches unto none, though somewhat late   50
Since burning aged women (save a few –
   Not witches only b——ches – who create
Mischief in families, as some know or knew,
   Should still be singed, but *slightly*, let me state),
Has been declared an act of inurbanity,
Malgré Sir Matthew Hales's great humanity.

8

Great Galileo was debarred the Sun,
   Because he fixed it; and, to stop his talking,
How Earth could round the solar orbit run,
   Found his own legs embargoed from mere walking: 60
The man was well-nigh dead, ere men begun
   To think his skull had not some need of caulking;
But now, it seems, he's right – his notion just:
No doubt a consolation to his dust.

9

Pythagoras, Locke, Socrates – but pages
  Might be filled up, as vainly as before,
With the sad usage of all sorts of sages,
  Who in his life-time, each, was deemed a Bore!
The loftiest minds outrun their tardy ages:
  This they must bear with and, perhaps, much more;   70
The wise man's sure when he no more can share it, he
Will have a firm Post Obit on posterity.

10

If such doom waits each intellectual Giant,
  We little people in our lesser way,
To Life's small rubs should surely be more pliant,
  And so for one will I – as well I may –
Would that I were less bilious – but, oh, fie on't!
  Just as I make my mind up every day,
To be a '*totus, teres,*' Stoic, Sage,
The wind shifts and I fly into a rage.   80

11

Temperate I am – yet never had a temper;
  Modest I am – yet with some slight assurance;
Changeable too – yet somehow '*Idem semper*':
  Patient – but not enamoured of endurance;
Cheerful – but, sometimes, rather apt to whimper:
  Mild – but at times a sort of '*Hercules furens*':
So that I almost think that the same skin
For one without – has two or three within.

12

Our Hero was, in Canto the Sixteenth,
  Left in a tender moonlight situation,   90
Such as enables Man to show his strength
  Moral or physical: on this occasion
Whether his virtue triumphed – or, at length,
  His vice – for he was of a kindling nation –
Is more than I shall venture to describe; –
Unless some Beauty with a kiss should bribe.

13

I leave the thing a problem, like all things: –
　　The morning came – and breakfast, tea and toast,
Of which most men partake, but no one sings.
　　The company whose birth, wealth, worth, have cost   100
My trembling Lyre already several strings,
　　Assembled with our hostess, and mine host;
The guests dropped in – the last but one, Her Grace,
The latest, Juan, with his virgin face.

14

Which best is to encounter – Ghost or none,
　　'Twere difficult to say – but Juan looked
As if he had combated with more than one,
　　Being wan and worn, with eyes that hardly brooked
The light, that through the Gothic windows shone:
　　Her Grace, too, had a sort of air rebuked –   110
Seemed pale and shivered, as if she had kept
A vigil, or dreamt rather more than slept.

[Here, the poem breaks off]

January 22nd 1824.
Messalonghi.
On this day I complete my thirty sixth year

1

'T is time this heart should be unmoved
　　Since others it hath ceased to move,
Yet though I cannot be beloved
　　Still let me love.

2

My days are in the yellow leaf
　　The flowers and fruits of love are gone –

The worm, the canker and the grief
    Are mine alone.

3

The fire that on my bosom preys
    Is lone as some Volcanic Isle,   10
No torch is kindled at its blaze
    A funeral pile!

4

The hope, the fear, the jealous care
    The exalted portion of the pain
And power of Love I cannot share
    But wear the chain.

5

But 't is not *thus* – and 't is not *here*
    Such thoughts should shake my soul, nor *now*
Where glory decks the hero's bier
    Or binds his brow.   20

6

The Sword – the Banner – and the Field
    Glory and Greece around us see!
The Spartan borne upon his shield
    Was not more free!

7

Awake! (*not* Greece – She *is* awake!)
    Awake my spirit – think through *whom*
Thy Life blood tracks its parent lake
    And then strike home!

8

Tread those reviving passions down
    Unworthy Manhood; – unto thee   30
Indifferent should the smile or frown
    Of Beauty be.

9

If thou regret'st thy youth, why *live?*
   The Land of honourable Death
Is here – up to the Field! and give
   Away thy Breath.

10

Seek out – less often sought than found,
   A Soldier's Grave – for thee the best,
Then look around and choose thy ground
   And take thy Rest.   40

['I watched thee']

1

I watched thee when the foe was at our side –
   Ready to strike at him, – or thee and me –
Were safety hopeless – rather than divide
   Aught with one loved – save love and liberty.

2

I watched thee in the breakers – when the rock
   Received our prow – and all was storm and fear,
And bade thee cling to me through every shock –
   This arm would be thy bark – or breast thy bier.

3

I watched thee when the fever glazed thine eyes –
   Yielding my couch – and stretched me on the ground –   10
When overworn with watching – ne'er to rise
   From thence – if thou an early grave hadst found.

4

The Earthquake came and rocked the quivering wall –
   And men and Nature reeled as if with wine –
Whom did I seek around the tottering Hall –
   For *thee* – whose safety first provide for – thine.

5

And when convulsive throes denied my breath
    The faintest utterance to my fading thought –
To thee – to thee – even in the grasp of death
    My spirit turned – Ah! oftener than it ought.   20

6

Thus much and more – and yet thou lov'st me not,
    And never wilt – Love dwells not in our will –
Nor can I blame thee – though it be my lot
    To strongly – wrongly – vainly – love thee still. –

[Last Words on Greece]

What are to me those honours or renown
    Past or to come, a new-born people's cry
Albeit for such I could despise a crown
    Of aught save Laurel, or for such could die;
I am the fool of passion – and a frown
    Of thine to me is an Adder's eye
To the poor bird whose pinion fluttering down
    Wafts unto death the breast it bore so high –
Such is this maddening fascination grown –
    So strong thy Magic – or so weak am I.   10

Notes

Abbreviations in notes: BLJ: *Byron's Letters and Journals*, ed. Leslie A. Marchand, 13 vols (London: John Murray, 1973–94).
CPW: Lord Byron, *The Complete Poetical Works*, ed. Jerome J. McGann (Oxford: Clarendon Press, 1980–93).

Inscription on the Monument of a Newfoundland Dog   Written 1808. Second part published 1809. B initially intended that 'Boatswain is to be buried in a vault waiting for myself' (BLJ, I, 178).

Farewell Petition to J[ohn] C[am] H[obhouse] Esq.   Written 1810. Published 1887. **2:** Hobhouse was at Cambridge with B and remained a close friend throughout his life. **6:** William Fletcher was B's manservant. **23–4:** two lines missing from CPW are here restored with grateful acknowledgement to John Murray. **32:** the mother of Elizabeth Pigot, a friend of B's adolescence. **33:** a pun on the name of George Sale, the orientalist. **34:** Longman: publishers; Hurst, Rees and Orme (48) are also publishers. **35:** Charles Skinner Matthews was a mutual Cambridge friend.

To Inez   Written 1810. Published 1812 in Canto I of *Childe Harold's Pilgrimage*.

Stanzas For Music   Written 1814. Published 1827–9.

She Walks in Beauty   Written 1814. Published 1815.

The Destruction of Semnacherib   Written and published 1815.

When We Two Parted   Written and published 1815.

Fare Thee Well!   Written and published 1816. The lines were addressed to Lady B in the hope of a reconciliation. **34:** Augusta Ada, B's only legitimate daughter (born 10 December 1815).

Endorsement to the Deed of Separation   Written 1816. Published 1830.

from **Childe Harold's Pilgrimage** Canto III   Written and published 1816. **Epigraph:** In order that this application will compel you to think of something else: there is in truth no remedy except that and time. **2:** Augusta Ada, B's daughter, was only a few weeks old when Lady B went away with her. B never saw his daughter again. **180:** Harmodius and Aristogeiton attempted to assassinate the tyrants of Athens with daggers concealed in myrtle. **181–216:** refers to a ball given by the Duchess of Richmond on 15 June 1816. **200:** Frederick Duke of Brunswick was killed at the Battle of Quatre Bras. **226:** clan song of the Camerons; Albyn (227) is the Gaelic name for Scotland. **227 Lochiel:** title of the Chief of the Camerons. **234:** Evan Cameron fought at Killiecrankie and Donald Cameron fought at Culloden. **316:** refers to Napoleon Buonaparte. **366 Philip's son:** Alexander the Great. **368 Diogenes:** founder of the Cynic school, he espoused an austere 'natural' life. **644 Lake Leman:** Lake Geneva. **848 Cytherea:** Aphrodite, Greek goddess of love; her girdle gave the wearer the power to attract love. **851–5:** the ancient Persians were believed to worship nature.

Sonnet on Chillon   Written and published 1816. B visited Chillon Castle by Lake Geneva with Shelley late June 1816. **13:** François Bonnivard was imprisoned in Chillon Castle 1530–6.

[Epistle to Augusta]   Written 1816. Published 1830. Augusta Leigh was B's half-sister with whom he had an intense and catastrophic relationship, in part responsible for the scandal of his separation from Lady B. **57:** B toured the Alps with Hobhouse September–October 1816. **73–4:** Newstead Abbey, Nottingham, B's English country house.

Darkness   Written and published 1816. Clouds caused by a volcanic eruption led to 1816 being 'the year without a summer'; B is also drawing on contemporary scientific discussions about global disaster. **50 clung:** shrunk, shrivelled.

from **Childe Harold's Pilgrimage** Canto IV   Written 1817. Published 1818. **8 winged Lion:** of St Mark's Square, Venice. **10 Cybele:** ancient mother-goddess of fertility and wild nature; she is often depicted surrounded by lions. **19 Tasso:** sixteenth-century Italian poet who was imprisoned for his political views and (allegedly) for his love of a nobleman's sister.

Venetian gondoliers used to recite his verses to each other. **31**: the last Doge
was deposed by the French in 1797 before the city passed into Austrian
control. **33 Shylock and the Moor**: characters in Shakespeare's *The
Merchant of Venice* and *Othello*. **34 Pierre**: character in Otway's *Venice
Preserved.* **1243–8**: the Colosseum, Rome. **1266 Dacian**: from the
territory north of the lower Danube; now Romania: Dacian prisoners are
depicted on Trajan's column and Constantine's Arch in Rome.
1378–1431: St Peter's in the Vatican Square, Rome. **1433–40**: Hellenis-
tic statue of Laocoon and his sons struggling with a serpent. **1441 Lord of
the unerring bow**: Roman statue known as Apollo Belvedere. **1672
sandal-shoon, and scallop-shell**: the traditional dress of pilgrims.

['So, We'll Go No More A Roving']   Written 1817. Published 1830. The
poem was part of a letter to Thomas Moore in which B reflected on his
participation in the Venetian carnival festivities and found '"the sword
wearing out the scabbard," though I have but just turned the corner of
twenty-nine' (BLJ, V, 176).

from Beppo, A Venetian Story   Written 1817–18. Published 1818. **337
becaficas**: small birds which feed on figs and grapes, eaten as a delicacy.
363: the painter Raphael was reputed to have died after energetic love-
making. **368**: Antonio Canova, contemporary Italian sculptor, famous for
classical lines. **369**: echoes William Cowper's patriotic concern in *The Task*,
II, 206. **371 lucubrate**: to compose or study late into the night.

from Don Juan   Written 1818–23. Published in separate volumes
1819–24.

Canto I (Published 1819)
754 Boscan, Garcilasso: sixteenth-century Spanish poets who imitated
Petrarch's sonnets. **773 Donna Inez**: Juan's mother (modelled in part on
Lady B). **807 Don Alfonso**: Julia's elderly husband. **829 Anacreon
Moore**: i.e. Thomas Moore who translated the Odes of Anacreon. **864
Louis**: a gold coin.

Canto II (Published 1819)
121–2: echoes Psalm 137. **127 portmanteau**: a travelling case often
lined with waste paper. **131**: quoting *Hamlet* V. 1. 240. **141 Guadalquivir**: Spanish river famously difficult for English tourists to pronounce. **1435
Xerxes**: king of Persia who mounted a huge invasion of Greece in 480.

1449: Haidee's father is absent. **1542 Stygian river:** the Styx, classical river of the Underworld across which the souls of the dead had to be ferried. **1563 Host:** consecrated bread in a Christian service of Eucharist. **1624:** Viscount Castlereagh was the English minister responsible for the repression of Irish Catholics and other harsh measures against reform. **1633–4:** Caesar was a suitor to Cleopatra, Antony was her slave; Titus mastered his passion for the Jewish Princess Berenice. **1635 Horace, Catullus, Ovid:** Roman writers who treated the theme of love as joyful, agonising, and a corrupt art respectively. **1636 Sappho:** Greek lyric poet famous for her passionate love songs about women and for throwing herself off the cliff of Leucas to cure unrequited love. **1638 Leucadia's rock:** on the Greek island of Leucas, suspected criminals were tried by being thrown over the island's high cliffs into the sea. If they survived, they were rescued and set free. **1643:** Caesar, Pompey, Mahomet and Belisarius were all believed to have endured their wives' marital infidelity. **1649 Epicurus:** Greek philosopher for whom pleasure was identical with good. **1650 Aristippus:** pupil of Socrates who believed that immediate pleasure was the only end of any action. **1656:** Sardanapalus was an Assyrian monarch who believed pleasure to be more important than military conquest. B wrote a tragedy about his overthrow. **1688 'beau ideal':** the perfect type of beauty. **1713 lazaret:** quarantine hospital, in the sense here of a store place.

Canto VIII (Published 1823)
7–8 Mars, Bellona: names for the Roman god and goddess of war. **13 Hydra:** Greek mythical many-headed snake. **34 Leonidas, Washington:** Spartan and American leaders famous for winning battles and being good men. **715 Pharisaic:** making a show of piety, self-righteous. **729 Cossacques:** Russians. **747 chirurgeons:** surgeons. **769 John Johnson:** the British mercenary soldier who befriended Juan in Canto V. **776 St George's collar:** B believed it to be a Russian military order. **777 Seraskier:** Turkish army commander-in-chief.

Canto IX (Published 1823)
8 'Nay!': pun on the name of Field Marshal Ney who fought bravely at Waterloo. **9–10:** Kinnaird received warning of an assassination attempt on Wellington but his attempts to protect the identity of his informant, Marinêt, were betrayed. **25:** quoting *Macbeth* III. 4. 16. **51 Cincinnatus:** legendary hero who saved the Roman army then went back to his farm. **55 Sabine farm:** for literary service to the Emperor Augustus, Horace was given a farm in the Sabine hills; Wellington had been given £500,000 after

Waterloo to purchase an estate. **58 Epaminondas:** brilliant military commander who led the Thebans against the Spartans but who died in poverty. **62:** Pitt refused to take money from the public purse to pay off his private debts and he introduced punitive levels of income tax to finance the wars with France. **105:** quoting *Hamlet* III. 1. 58. **107 Alexander:** the Great: Hephaestion was his companion from childhood. **113:** B translates Horace's mock heroic invective against garlic. **129:** Montaigne's essays were prefixed with the motto: 'What do I know?' **138 Pyrrho:** founder of philosophical scepticism who advocated withholding judgement about all things. **145:** quoting *Othello* II. 3. 95; 103–4. **149:** quoting *Hamlet* V. 2. 165–6. **153 Theogony:** study of the genealogy of deities in heathen mythology. **158 Lykanthropy:** form of insanity in which sufferers believe themselves to be wolves. **162 Moses:** long-suffering leader of the Jews in the Old Testament; **Melancthon:** a German humanist, famous for his tolerance.

Canto XI (Published 1823)

441–2: Moscow, Leipsic, Mont Saint Jean were all military defeats for Napoleon. *Marino Faliero* and *Cain* (1821) were literary 'defeats' for B. **448:** Sir Hudson Lowe supervised Napoleon's detention on St Helena. **449:** refers to the writers Sir Walter Scott, Thomas Moore, Thomas Campbell. **454:** the productive Rev. George Croly, an author and critic, is likened to Cambyses, king of Persia who conquered Egypt. **456:** quoting *I Henry IV* II. 5. 210. **460:** name of a character with ox-like abilities; *dorsuarius* = that carries a load on its back. **461 Sporus:** effeminate favourite of the Emperor Nero. **463–4: roaring Romans** refers to Croly's play *Catiline*; **howling Hebrews** refers to Henry Hart Milman's *The Fall of Jerusalem*. **465 Euphues:** a character associated with affectation invented by John Lyly. B refers to Barry Cornwall who produced a 'gentler' sort of *ottava rima*. **471 Boeotian:** the writer Walter Savage Landor is likened to the inhabitants of Boetia in ancient Greece, who were proverbially dim-witted. **473:** refers to the myth that John Keats suffered a haemorrhage after reading a hostile review of his poems. **487–8 thirty tyrants:** refers to the power struggle in the reign of Gallienus. **490 Praetorian:** refers to the disorderly period when the Praetorians (imperial bodyguards) auctioned off Rome to the highest bidder. **491:** quoting *King Lear* IV. 5. 15. **495 Janizaries:** escort guards (Turkish). **516 Centaur-Nessus:** the wife of Hercules gave him a robe smeared with the blood of a centaur, Nessus, in the belief that this charm would win back his love: the robe was poisoned and Hercules died in agony. **536 Or Molu:** gilded bronze decoration. **548 Jack Horner:** a popular nursery rhyme begins 'Little Jack Horner sat in the corner . . .' **560 quadrille:** a dance performed by four couples. **572 bogle:** a phantom or ghost (Scottish). **573 crupper:** rump of a horse. **590 rack and manger:** rack and ruin; waste and destruction. **601:** Byron refers to the general theme of 'Resignation: in Two Parts', a poem Edward Young wrote when about eighty years old. **611:** Henry Grattan and John Philpot Curran were Whig statesmen. Richard Brinsley Sheridan was a playwright and former drinking companion of B's. **613–14:** Queen Caroline suffered a scandalous investigation into her character in 1820; Princess Charlotte's death in childbirth in 1817 caused national mourning. **615 Five per Cents:** interest on British bonds whose value fluctuated on the stock exchange. **617–18:** Beau Brummell and William Long Pole Wellesley were well-known Regency dandies. Samuel Whitbread was a leading Whig politician, Sir Samuel Romilly had been solicitor-general and he represented Lady B in the separation proceedings. **620 'Fum' the Fourth:** refers to Thomas Moore's satire on George IV in which 'Fum' was a Chinese bird of royalty, decorating the Brighton Pavilion. **631 the Grenvilles:** an eminent family well known for shifts of political allegiance. **633:** Lady Caroline Lamb and Lady Frances Wedderburn Webster had romantic affairs with Byron and others; they both eventually left their husbands. **636:** the *Morning Post* was a newspaper which reported high society scandal. **661 blue Peter:** a nautical flag signalling immediate sailing. **666 Johanna Southcote:** a visionary prophetess from Devonshire whose sect attracted a substantial following in the early nineteenth century. **670:** B was sceptical about the Congress of Verona (1822). **681 'Carpe diem':** from Horace meaning 'seize the present day'. **683 harpy:** a mythical beast part bird, part woman; a greedy and rapacious person. **685:** quoting *Macbeth* V. 5. 23 and *I Henry IV* II. 5. 489. **693 Atalantis:** after an eighteenth-century novel exposing scandal from high life, any secret or scandalous history.

Canto XVI (Published 1824)
931 'sans culotte': without breeches; term for a supporter of the French Revolution. **960 tête-à-tête:** face to face, in an intimate situation. **966 tympanum:** ear-drum. **970–1:** from Dante's *Inferno*: Abandon hope all you who enter here. **997 carte and tierce:** fencing terms for the fourth (quarte) and third (terce) positions for thrusting and parrying. **1032 FitzFulke:** one of the other guests; her surname has a sexual connotation.

Canto XVII (Left unfinished when B went to Greece. Published 1903.)
48: Luther questioned the doctrines of the Catholic Church. **52 bitches:**

hints directed at Lady B's servant whom B blamed for encouraging their separation. **56**: Sir Matthew Hale presided over some seventeenth-century witchcraft trials. **57**: Galileo was imprisoned by order of the Inquisition for advocating the then heretical Copernican theory of planetary movement. **65**: Pythagoras and Socrates were intellectual martyrs; Locke was temporarily expelled from England for his political beliefs. **72 Post Obit:** taking effect after someone's death. **77 bilious:** suffering from excess bile; ill-tempered. **79 *'totus, teres':*** from Horace, 'wholly smooth and rounded', even-tempered. **83 *'Idem semper':*** always the same, constant. **86 *'Hercules furens':*** the title of a tragedy about the madness of Hercules.

January 22nd 1824   Written 1824. Published 1824.

['I watched thee']   Written 1824. Published 1887. The poem is addressed to the fifteen-year-old Greek boy, Loukas Chalandritsanos, with whom B was passionately in love. **13**: the earthquake at Missolonghi was on 21 February 1824.

[Last words on Greece]   Written 1824. Published 1824.